introduction to
DOCUMENTARY PRODUCTION

WALLFLOWER PRESS LONDON & NEW YORK

First published in Great Britain in 2002 by Wallflower Press
5 Pond Street, Hampstead, London NW3 2PN
www.wallflowerpress.co.uk

A catalogue record for this book is available from the British Library

ISBN 1 903364 37 X (paperback)
ISBN 1 903364 46 9 (hardback)

Book design by Rob Bowden Design

Printed in Great Britain by Antony Rowe Ltd, Chippenham, Wiltshire

contents

acknowledgements

I would like to express my thanks first and foremost to the contributors who put up with my suggestions and nagging for the best part of a year. Many thanks also to the University of Portsmouth administration staff, especially Maureen Dewey and Jenny Keam, for their fabulous support. Finally, thanks to Tracey Flintoff at the University of Portsmouth, Christine Lloyd Lyons at the Kobal Collection, and Alison Gordon at Sky publicity for all their recommendations and help in the provision of photographs.

Searle Kochberg
July 2002

notes on contributors

colin denahy is a senior technical manager in production and post-production at the University of Portsmouth. Prior to joining the University, he worked for many years in television production in the UK.

william garrison works as a producer in the learning development centre at the University of Portsmouth. His background is in terrestrial programme making in the US and UK, and his current work focuses on new media/streaming media.

ron geesin researches into sound at the University of Portsmouth. His work experience includes documentary production and feature film, both of which have benefitted from his original sound scores and compositions.

janice kearns teaches in the media section of the University of Portsmouth where she lectures in professional practice and production management. She has worked as a production manager on many independent productions for Channel 4, the BBC and ITV in the UK.

searle kochberg heads the BA in Video Production at the University of Portsmouth where he lectures in film/television theory and practice. He has written on the American and British film industries and regularly contributes to film magazines.

damian toal teaches video production at the University of Portsmouth. He is a freelance editor and programme maker with many years experience, and is an installation and performance-based video artist.

marie womack teaches media studies at the University of Portsmouth. Her background is in performance and both print and radio journalism. She is currently researching into audiences, media and dance.

jane young teaches documentary production at the University of Portsmouth. Her extensive media experience includes working as a producer and director of non-fiction programming for television companies and government institutions in the UK.

introduction searle kochberg

In the UK and elsewhere, documentary production is a central focus of many pre-Degree and Degree courses in Media. The University of Portsmouth, where I teach, is no exception.

This book is an attempt to introduce a systematic approach to concepts – creative, technical and theoretical – that inform documentary production at college. Involved as we are in academia and the media industry, we, the contributors, have taken it upon ourselves to summarise these concepts in ways accessible to students new to documentary, for whom the subject may appear at once deceptively straightforward, and a logistics and ethical minefield. To facilitate clear understanding, we have incorporated case studies to bring out the points we are making.

All involved in this book are committed to documentaries that demonstrate the ethic of responsibility. We recognise that truths are subjective, multiple and at times contradictory. So we do not suggest that you aspire to the impossible – the rendition of the truth – but rather that you see as valuable and achievable the articulation of a truth in your work that illuminates and informs in an exciting way. In this sense we are clearly not postmodernists. For us, structure and rhetorical devices – cinematography, sound, editing – are there to help you fashion your arguments, and we remain positive to the force of documentary work which is grounded in ethical rigour and which represents some version of actuality and experience.

The chapters in the book are placed in an order that reflects the process of making and illuminates key issues as they arise during pre-production, production and post-production.

Chapter 1, by Jane Young, looks at the key issue of content in documentary: i.e. concept, structure and script. Through examples from her own career and elsewhere, Jane makes the point that there is no single approach to structure and script. These processes occur to a greater or lesser degree, and earlier or later in the production, depending on the project at hand and the conceptual framework behind it.

Chapter 2, by Searle Kochberg, continues to explore structural patterns by considering narrativity and intent in documentary. In a number of classic and contemporary examples of film and television documentary, the chapter also explores rhetorical style using the classification introduced by Bill Nichols, and considers individual versus institutional authorship.

Chapter 3, by Marie Womack, deals with the concept of audiences and documentary programming, looking at specific examples of construction and targeting of audiences, and notions of audience gratification/pleasure. Marie ends the chapter by speculating on 'active' participation in meaning by audiences in the light of New Media.

Chapter 4, by Janice Kearns, shifts the focus beyond research and development to production management – budgeting, scheduling, location work, contingencies, copyright – from pre-production, through production to post-production. Janice illuminates her arguments by citing examples from her career in broadcasting.

Chapter 5, by William Garrison, looks at practical applications of cinematography in documentary production. He encourages non-fiction makers to use a wide spectrum of techniques in their documentaries, and, in tandem with Searle Kochberg's earlier

01 **structure and script** jane young

In this chapter, above all else, I want to stress the importance of structure. Although by definition non-fiction film-making deals with existing material, there still needs to be a narrative structure. The main differences between non-fiction and fiction structure lie in how the structure is imposed. Precisely because non-fiction film deals with existing material, there are available to the non-fiction film-maker a huge range of ready-made shaping devices for his/her film. These include authorial voice, time and place, events, process, institution and existing texts. However, many of these structures and shaping devices cannot be fully documented until they occur, and this has huge implications for the scripting process. Unlike fiction, the non-fiction film maker does not have complete control over her/his material. The maker is, therefore, not always able to produce a detailed script before production.

This chapter is in five sections. First we look at the importance of deciding the concept, which will have huge implications for how the structure is defined. This is discussed in the next section. Here we show, through case studies, some of the options available. The section after that addresses what this book will identify as the key issues: truth/construction, aesthetics/interpretation, ethics and the role of the maker. Essentially it examines the implications these issues have on the choice of structure, again through case studies. The fourth section deals with developing the script, and details the stages of proposal, treatment, storyboard, shooting schedule and paper edit. The most pragmatic section of the five, it details the requirements for each stage and stresses their importance. The final section summarises the concerns of the chapter and provides innovative guidelines for the non-fiction film-maker. Essentially it will show how the nature of the structure will prescribe the timing and development of the script.

DECIDING THE CONCEPT

Non-fiction film-making serves a huge variety of purposes. These include promotion, propaganda, investigation, education, entertainment and the dissemination of information. However, with the advent of affordable digital technology, the concept of producing non-fiction film as a form of creative self-expression is becoming much more of a reality. This chapter assumes that this desire to interpret reality creatively is the main purpose of the aspiring non-fiction film-makers to whom it is addressed.

Creative self-expression means that there is no initial directive from a commissioning group. And though not working to a specific brief may seem liberating, very often the reverse is true. So in any discussion of structure and script, defining the specific concept must come first. What will the film be about, and what do you want to say about it?

It is not enough to decide to make a film 'about' homeless people, scooters, performance* artists, football supporters, breast cancer, urban landscapes, or your relationship with your parents. Any one of these subjects lends itself to a huge variety of interpretations – which one do you want to communicate to your audience? What is your view? How do you want to represent your subject and what story do you want to tell? You must have what Michael Rabiger, in his definitive text *Directing the Documentary,* calls a 'working hypothesis' (1998: 133–5).

So your position on homelessness might be that many older men deliberately choose to live rough, enjoy their independence, and work the system at the expense of the tax payer. Conversely (and more likely, given the natural predilection of film-makers to identify sympathetically with their subjects) you might want to portray them as victims of an indifferent society which is incapable of responding to the needs of individuals. Either concept is an acceptable working hypothesis, containing a strongly stated position which can be developed in the film. In short, your film must have both a subject, and clearly identified themes. Without clearly defined themes, there is a real danger that the film will be no more than a montage of 'look at life' images glued together either by music or a voice-over narration – visual wallpaper with nothing

figure 1
something's happening

particular to say and no story to tell. However, once you are clear about what it is you want to communicate to your audience, deciding how to structure the film becomes an informed and exciting decision-making process which will enable you to collect material in a way that will be appropriate to the story you want to tell. Then and only then is it possible to consider how the story can be told – what its organizing rationale and structure will be.

DEFINING THE STRUCTURE

What, then, are the most important structuring elements in non-fiction film-making? It seems to me that these must be the events and activities that engage your subject during the time that you are able to film. This is the crucial distinction between fiction and non-fiction production. Though both forms involve narrative patterning, in non-fiction film-making the raw-material does not have to be created from your imagination, it already exists – or will exist. So the first thing you need to research, having determined your subject and what you want to say about it, is 'what will happen that I can film?'

Structuring your film is essentially a very practical activity, arising from intensive research into the nature of your chosen subjects. Imagine you have decided to make a film about two jazz musicians, who are pensioners. Your working hypothesis is that their shared obsession with music transcends the infirmities of old age. As this is one of your graduation films, you have a period of two to three months in which to film. You have found out that the subjects play music on the street most Wednesdays and Saturdays, and are also heavily in demand for private functions. You have been to their house and it is a treasure trove of jazz memorabilia. For the structure to take on substance and clarity, you now need to find out what will happen during those three months which will illustrate your working hypothesis. Moving house, practising for a special function, going on holiday, are all events you can plan around. Getting ill, being ousted from their favourite pitch, falling out with other members, will be things that you cannot plan for – but it would be wise to make contingencies for their occurrence.

Molly Dineen's film about Geri Halliwell, *Geri* (RTO for C4, 1999) charts the struggle of a superstar to find her own separate identity over a period of months, and shows how a structure can evolve from a combination of set-piece events (becoming UN ambassador, singing at Prince Charles' birthday) and domestic situations (chatting with her mum in the kitchen, seeing her new house, buying a puppy). So available events and activities are crucial elements that define your structure. Inextricably linked to this are decisions that you must take about the handling of time and place. Indeed it is this sense of time and place that gives a non-fiction film a narrative structure.

The development of time will largely be determined by the amount of time you have to make your production, and the treatment of place is dependant on budget, accessibility and again, time. All too often in student films there is no sense of time or place at all – the sounds and images are presented in a vacuum which could be anywhere, and any time of the day or year.

Time is central to the development of the characters, the action, the story. At one extreme, as in Michael Apted's seminal documentary series *7 Up*, the passage of time has so far covered fifty years as key characters are revisited every seven years, providing the main structuring device. Similarly, in his series of documentaries for the BBC entitled *The Visit* (1982–91 and 1993–94) Desmond Wilcox followed his subject through life-changing experiences and follow-up visits. Conversely, that old school essay favourite 'a day in the life of...' has provided the structure for non-fiction films as diverse in concept as *Every Day Except Christmas* (Graphic Films, 1957), Lindsay Anderson's observational study of working Britain, at Covent Garden market, *One Day in September* (Passion Pictures, 1999), Kevin Macdonald's Oscar-winning documentary about the killing of 11 Israeli competitors at the Olympic games, and *London* (2000), Angus McQueen's film for the BBC2 series *Modern Times* in which

figure 2
when to structure

23 camera crews simultaneously record a breathtaking variety of parallel activities during one day in the city.

Essentially there needs to be some kind of development in time – some kind of before and after progression – for your film to tell a story. Even if this progression is based on events from the past, as in any personal story or historical reconstruction, there must be a sense of time unfolding. Often film-makers feel inspired to make non-fiction films about ordinary people, often with an obsession that marks them out as individual – for example fast cars, tattoos, stamp-collecting. The key questions to ask yourself are 'what do I want to say about them?' (the working hypothesis) and 'what will happen to them?' (what is the timescale?). I made a film about six Portsmouth football supporters (*End of Terrace*, BBC2, 1994) and the tricky bit of the structure was 'how will they develop?' It is relatively easy to put together a feature showing what somebody is like – it is much harder to get the audience to follow them in a journey through time, where there will be some sort of change and/or resolution.

A sense of place, too, helps tell a story. Do we feel we know the location as well as if we had been there ourselves? Sometimes the place is also the subject of the film, as in Sasha Snow's beautiful documentary about the St Petersburg Library, *A St Petersburg Symphony* (National Film School, 2000). Here the silence and serenity of the building, contrasted with the deprivation of living conditions outside, provides a metaphor for the courage and resilience of the people who work in it. Even when there are a wide variety of locations, as in *Listen to Britain* (Humphrey Jennings, Crown Film Unit, 1942), where apparently unconnected activities all over the country are woven into a lyrical sound poem, there should be an overarching concept of place – in this case wartime Britain.

Most key locations in a film will need to be recorded in at least two different times of day or weather conditions for the audience to get any sense of the essential nature of the place – this will also tie in with the development in time.

Activities and events, and the treatment of time and location within them are key elements of structure. Over and above these however, you should consider the possibility of finding a metaphorical device which can both illustrate your working hypothesis and provide a parallel structure to the film. Angus McQueen's *Vodka* (BBC2, 2000) intersperses his telling account of a Russia befuddled by drink with a moral fairytale. Laura Green's *A Quick Thrill* (Portsmouth graduation film, 2000) uses parallel cutting of a rollercoaster ride as the metaphor for her interpretation of Wednesday night in the students' bar... In the slide installation about my father, *The Life* (1999), I used four simultaneous narratives. They were my story, my father's story, generalised sequences of parents and children as they grew up, and a journey of a brook to the sea, which provided a metaphor for the other three.

Consider, too, the use of existing text to provide structure. In the classic *Night Mail* (GPO film unit, 1936) Basil Wright uses W. H. Auden's poem of the same name to underpin the journey of the train from London to Edinburgh. Music can provide a potent and unifying structure when it is creatively interpreted and is appropriate to the story. One of the most powerful sequences in Michael Moore's *Roger and Me* (Dog Eat Dog Films, 1989) comes when a worker from General Motors describes listening to the Beachboys' song 'Wouldn't it Be Nice?' after he has been laid off. This same song is then played over rows and rows of repossessed empty property making a powerful and ironic statement.

We have identified the main structuring elements as events and activities, time, place and metaphor. Once you have identified the events and activities you want to film, decide how you are going to handle time and place, and explore the possibilities of metaphor in the form of icons or parallel activities – then you can revisit your concept and start to structure your film.

It is worth noting some basic characteristics of narrative structure, without which it is extremely difficult to communicate your message. Stories need to have a beginning, a middle and an end. Your film should introduce your subject and make clear what it is you want to say about it. There should then be some sense of development, which generates a narrative tension (what will happen?). In most instances there should also be a feeling of resolution, or closure at the end (we know what to think). If your concept and structuring elements have been clearly defined and identified, using them to create a narrative should be like fitting pieces of jigsaw puzzle together.

So much then for ways of deciding how to structure the film. But what criteria will influence your decision? This brings us on to the next section – the key issues to address when deciding on structure.

KEY ISSUES TO ADDRESS

Before we move on to the relationship of structure to script, there are some fundamental issues that need to be resolved. These issues are addressed throughout this book – and are as crucial to the development of structure as to any other aspect of production.

The role of the film-maker

The very nature of the production process, with editorial decision-making at every stage, presupposes that any non-fiction film will be a subjective, creative interpretation of truths. However, the perceived role of the film-maker will vary, depending on how personal you want to make it, and how much you want the audience to realise that this is your subjective view. As a general rule, the more overtly personal/subjective the film, the greater the role in the structuring process. This authorial voice can be imposed in a variety of ways.

Chris Marker in *Sans Soleil* (Argos Films, 1983) uses a woman's voice reading from letters apparently written by him ('he wrote me that...') to record his observations on the visual material he collected in his journeys round the world. Dziga Vertov in *Man with a Movie Camera* (Vufku, 1929) makes a highly anti-realist and reflexive interpretation of the life of a city (Kiev). Both are devices for communicating the authorial voice. Film-makers like Michael Moore and Nick Broomfield make explicit their authorial voice by making the structure their attempts to interview their subjects. See, for instance, *Roger and Me* and *The Leader, the Driver and the Leader's Wife* (Lafayette Films, 1991).

Conversely, Frederick Wiseman keeps himself out of his films, which are structured not by commentary or interventionist confrontations (for the most part) but by painstakingly documented and edited narrative sequences which give the impression of unfolding reality.

Incidentally, the role of the film-maker should not be confused with the role of presenter, which is another structuring device used by film-makers to manipulate their material.

Aesthetics/naturalism

In the same way that an audience will accept the presence or authorial voice of the film-maker if it is clearly a personal project, so they will accept (and indeed expect) an aesthetic which creatively interprets that vision. Thus the use of black and white, sepia, slow motion, and the whole range of effects that are now available in digitised* post-production are invaluable devices if used appropriately to communicate your identified themes.

However, if your aim is to present a story in as observational and apparently naturalistic a way as possible, then your aesthetic approach should keep the effects down to a minimum.

Truth

What role does truth play in the structuring process?

Given the editorial nature of the process, a documentary/non-fiction film can only ever represent a truth, selected by you the film-maker. It is my contention that all really effective non-fiction films contain at least one narrative moment which sums up the essence of the themes and truths that the film-maker wants to reveal about his or her subject. Just as Harold Evans, in his anthology of great news photographs *Pictures on a Page*, defines them as recording a 'key moment' (1997: 72), so all non-fiction film-makers who are passionate about their work will try to capture a sequence or reaction that encapsulates a truth that they want the audience to see about the story they are telling. These moments are hard to get, because they can only come when the social actors* of the film have forgotten about the camera, or at any rate are not performing to the camera. They should also be reacting to, or reflecting on, events not related to the production of the film. Great story-telling non-fiction moments, for me, include the children playing in the streets in Salford (*Morning in the Streets*, Denis Mitchell, BBC,

1959), Tony the ex-jockey telling his wife he's been unfaithful (*35 Up*, Michael Apted, Granada Television, 1991) and Craig finding out that Nick has been telling lies (*Big Brother*, Bazal Productions for C4, 2000). If you are clever and lucky enough to record a story-telling sequence that sums up decisively your working hypothesis – that is, the truth that you want to show – then you will have the key moment of your narrative structure.

Ethics

The general public are becoming increasingly wary about agreeing to be subjects of non-fiction film-making, and rightly so. Over the last few years a multitude of docu-soaps and factual disaster movies have misrepresented people in a variety of staged or sensationalised stereotypes. While the purpose of non-fiction film-making is not to provide a promotional video for its subjects, and all editorial decision-making should lie with the film-maker, at the same time there is a clear ethical duty not to misrepresent people.

In terms of the structuring process the implications are straightforward; make sure that the story you want to tell about your subject is one that they would agree is not a misrepresentation. They may not be particularly happy with how they are presented, but – in my opinion – they should be able to agree that it is a justifiable interpretation.

DEVELOPING THE SCRIPT

Having analysed the elements and issues surrounding structure, we now need to examine the implications this has for the paperwork. In non-fiction film-making the extent to which the structure can initially be expressed on paper depends on the predictability of the material. If the structure is largely determined by recording events and activities as they unfold, then clearly it will not be possible to produce a detailed script in the same way that we would, say, for a drama. However, there are a number of stages in the production of any non-fiction film which need to be committed to paper – not only to convince potential commissioners that it is worth backing, but also to clarify your intentions for yourself and your crew.

The first stage is the proposal. This should be no more than a sheet of A4 and should sum up your concept. What are the subjects of your film? What is your working hypothesis? How will you say it?

Since this single sheet of paper will need to grab the attention of whoever reads it, it must paint visual pictures and convey – in short, clear sentences – how and why the audience will be affected by the story that you have to tell. The writing should be in the present tense and get to the heart of the issues immediately. Here is the first paragraph of a proposal for a film about the way tattooing has become a mainstream activity, written in a way guaranteed to send any commissioning editor to sleep.

I have been very interested in the rather complicated, and some might say potentially painful art of tattooing for some time, and have long wanted to make a film about it. The film that I propose will examine the history, process and increasingly popular activity of tattooing in a way that will bring this whole subject vividly to life.

Compare that with this:

Tracey Evans is 14 and this Saturday she's going downtown to get John Craven to tattoo a butterfly on her shoulder. This is nothing new for John; in the past few years his trade has seen a shift from muscled dockworkers through punks to teenyboppers – tattoos have gone mainstream. But Tracey's mum doesn't know about it, Tracey herself has a low pain threshold, and that butterfly won't come off in the wash. *Skin Deep* begins with John in his shop on Saturday and finds out how he reconciles these issues.

Proposals should indicate some elements of structure and show how the narrative will develop. They should also show that you are capable of producing the film and indicate your preferred deadlines for the production. Where possible include photographs and quotations from your subjects. It should be possible to write a proposal after initial research and when a firm decision on your concept has been reached.

A treatment, however, can only be written after the structure has been very clearly defined, and all events and activities and places to be filmed have, where possible, been identified and decisions in the handling of time and possible metaphors, icons and parallel actions have been made. This is because treatments need to be much more detailed – usually between 4–8 pages – and should contain an introductory synopsis and a detailed description of each section of the project. There must be evidence of thorough research: names, locations, descriptions, actions and historic references which bring the content of the project to life. Writing must be in the present tense and accessible, and if nothing else the opening sequence, transitions and conclusions should be clearly and vividly articulated. Like the proposal, the treatment is vital if you need to convince outside parties to sponsor or commission your work. Students who have crew, equipment and film at their disposal will understand this more forcibly only once they leave college.

The treatment also fulfils another function; to clarify and peg down your narrative structure. It forces you to visualise the film in great detail before production takes place, thus greatly increasing the chances of recording appropriate and telling material at the right time. Most treatments will go through a number of drafts in pre-production.

Here is the first page of a treatment for the film about the jazz singers. You will see it deals with the themes of the film and how they are expressed in the narrative structure, as it develops in the first minute of the film in some detail.

figure 3
a story to tell

INTRO ... fade up from black ... A hot summer day in the cathedral city of Chichester. Crowds of shoppers and holiday-makers throng the pedestrianised cobbled streets, stroll through the cathedral precinct, rendezvous and congregate at the ancient stone cross in the centre ... sun filters through the leaves of the huge plane trees and glints on the cathedral spire. Caption: 'Chichester Summer 2000'. The strains of a saxophone play over close shots of shoppers pausing, stopping, their attention caught ... cut to a big close up of the horn of a saxophone. The camera slowly travels up the instrument until it stops on a BCU of Bryn Lewis, 70-year-old sax player, eyes closed, battered fedora on his head, immersed in the music; we hear the voice of his wife, Phyl: 'With Bryn – it's total commitment. I always say – I think of that saxophone as an extension of his body' ... The camera pans right and pulls focus to show in mid-shot Phyl Lewis, a small red-haired woman in her sixties with high heels, scarves and lots of jewellery. She is holding the microphone close and singing *Summertime* to a rapidly increasing crowd. Behind her is the drummer, also in his sixties, and beyond that the white-haired double bass player. In voice over we hear Bryn say: 'I've got an entry in my diary that says "Formed new band, signed drummer and female vocalist!" And then a bit later on it says ... "Married vocalist".' A series of reverse close shots of individual people in the audience – a three-year-old swinging on his mother's arm in time to the music, an old lady in a wheelchair – finally a middle-aged man listening intently. Phyl in voice over: 'People say to me "I bring my husband into town on a Wednesday or a Saturday and he says 'You go and do the shopping and I'll stay and listen to the band'".' Wide shot from behind the crowd showing how it has grown dissolves to CU of leaves of plane trees and glimpses of sunbathers in cathedral grounds ... strains of *Summertime* become fainter. Phyl in voice over: 'We didn't think last summer, did we, how tough the next six months were going to be...'

Fade to black ... Bring up title: MR AND MRS BRYN LEWIS ARE MOVING.

Key characters, activities, the handling of time and place, and metaphoric devices should all be covered in a complete treatment. Linked with this are detailed storyboards of particular sequences which take shape only during the process of writing the treatment.

The next stage in scripting occurs as the project moves into production, and consists of call sheets, shooting schedules and shot lists every time material is recorded. The Appendices at the end of this chapter include examples from the 'jazz singers film' and assume resources to be those of a student, rather than those of a commercially funded production. Note the amount of practical information and the way the themes of the film are spelled out to the crew, so that at every stage they are aware of the kind of shots the director is looking for. This will enable the camera operator to use his or her own creative initiative and get on with the job more effectively.

The final stages of paperwork are the logging and transcribing of material and the paper edit. Logging and transcribing of tapes/film stock should be done as soon as material is recorded, rather than left to post-production. There are really no hard and fast rules as to how it should be done so long as audio and video are noted separately – this will be vital for the paper edit.

In effect, the paper edit should be a realisation of the treatment, and will also result from the translation of recorded activities, use of time, space and metaphor into the identified themes of the concept. One useful method of organising this material is to identify everything from the logged transcripts in terms of the already defined structure. So, at its most basic, the introduction, conclusion and relevant sections should each have identified material assigned to them. Then and only then is it possible to do a detailed paper edit which will include time codes, not forgetting the audio in and out points not in vision, and any other material – for example stills, found footage, graphics – to be included. Again, there is no set rule for how to do this, but it must be possible to read video and audio separately, and to allow for at least four audio tracks and two video tracks to run concurrently.

WAYS OF WORKING

So much, then, for the different stages of the script. As we have already noted, the extent to which the structure can initially be expressed on paper depends on the predictability of the material. In this final section we look in more detail at how the type of structure will determine the stage at which the script is most clearly defined.

Firstly, there are the non-fiction films whose structure enables them to have a script/story board that is as detailed as that of a fiction film. These are films where an already existing text provides the fixed structure, making the script/story board a matter of interpretation. The text may take the form of a scripted commentary or poem, as in *Night Mail*, where Auden's words provide a rhythm and inspiration for the images. It may be a simple structural device, such as the alphabet or numbers (many of Peter Greenaway's early satires of documentary film are structured as catalogues in this way) or it may even be a piece of music. In *The Life*, I interpreted the second movement of Beethoven's Symphony No 6 to tell four different non-fiction narratives simultaneously. To do this I scripted and storyboarded all four stories to the music so that each narrative was made up of 160 images with the same edit points, which were then able to be projected on four screens simultaneously, each narrative with its own mixed soundtrack. Without such a detailed structure at pre-production this would not have been possible.

Generally, where the film-maker has a clear creative vision, and the film she/he wants to make has elements of poetic interpretation – particularly where an existing text is used – then detailed scripting comes at an early stage.

In non-fiction films where an actuality provides the structure – where the linear development is logical and straightforward and the film is edited to give the impression of 'real time', then the most detailed scripting tends to come at the actual production stage. In other words, the shooting schedules that are produced to provide explicit direction to the crew recording events and activities will form the basis for the final film.

21

Examples of this are non-fiction films where the structure takes the form of a journey, or a quest, or a 'day in the life'. The success or failure of such films lies in the content and quality of the actuality that is recorded.

Finally there are those non-fiction films which are issue-based and/or have a structure which is determined by the subjective interpretation of the film-maker to the events they have recorded. The detailed scripting here usually occurs in post-production.

Where a film-maker – such as Frederick Wiseman or Molly Dineen – sets out to interpret their subjects in a particular way, they will need to amass a huge amount of material which then needs an intensive and creative paper-edit. These are films which use actuality as the raw material from which they are created. The films' underlying meanings are conveyed by the selection and juxtaposition of the sounds and images, and this is a process that can only happen once the material is recorded. Very often a paper edit will go through a number of drafts, and the editing process will be a long and painful one with constant revision.

What this chapter has attempted to show is the relationship of structure to script in non-fiction film. I have assumed throughout that we are dealing with the production of linear film or video. However, the introduction of new technologies has meant that the designing of interactive structures for non-fiction production is becoming a commercial reality.

Although beyond the scope of this chapter, this area of Moving Image is too important not to mention briefly here. The key difference in terms of structure lies in the realisation that the audience is able to explore parallel narratives, make comparisons and connections for themselves, and construct their own time values. Therefore there is a new and over-ridingly important consideration to be made in the structuring process. This is the identification of common elements which can act as triggers for stand-alone narrative sequences. As digital technology, video streaming and interactivity become the norm, the importance of structure in non-fiction film is greater than ever.

APPENDIX A

Call sheet for Tuesday Oct 17th

JY dir; J O'G camera; SB sound

Relevant phone nos and addresses

Equipment

J's 3 chip mini dv camcorder

Manfrotto tripod

Sennheiser mic

Headphones ... no lights

reflector if poss, if not silver foil

J to remember ... Charge batteries – only 71 mins, get another if poss

Supply 1.5v batteries for mic + dv tapes

White card for white balance

Money for train fares

Check out Phil on sat for final schedule on tues

J to try and get equipment on Mon. If not possible till Tues then JG can be picked up same time – around 9.00am. Otherwise JG and SB to get train to Chichester to be met by J by 9.45am.

If we can get more batteries or we can use the old house power supply we could get a couple of hours' worth spread over the day. More likely and more cost effective we can get the shots we need in the morning – just over an hour's worth.

Transport J's car. Lunch supplied by J. Parking is OK and cleared with the building supervisor.

Shooting Schedule

Outline map showing position of houses, points of compass, position of sun, and relevant key camera positions.

At the moment I'm not quite sure how the removal van will get from A to B or when. They will be arriving at the old house at 9.00am and there's still some packing to be done. I'm estimating that if we get there around 10.00am everyone will still be in the old house and we can get the shots we need there then go with them to the new house and get the rest. We will have to wait until they are ready to do the actual move so hope that's soon. Alternatively I'll know by Saturday if they're hoping to be in the new house before then. If they are, we'll have to turn up at 9.00am at the latest.

The main purpose of this shoot is to record a crucial moment in their lives. We want to show the main themes of the film – that music is their shared obsession in life – that they have an indomitable spirit, fuelled by their love for music and each other – and that this is the end of an era and maybe the beginning of a new one.

APPENDIX B

Shot list

A. Old House

1) Emotive cutaways

       Empty rooms

       Faded patches on walls espec. front room.

Int: music room

       Pan round music room

       Shot up empty stairs and down

       Empty kitchen

Ext: Apple tree with fallen leaves in back garden

       back looking into music room with B and P in it

Ext: front

       Empty milk bottles

       Old front door BCU dilapidated frame

Tyre marks of Volvo

2) Action sequence

Int*:   B & P looking round inside music room

          'saying goodbye'

          Minimum 3 shot variation

          So as well as main MLS of action, CUs of ... Faces, artefacts

Ext*:   Removal men packing up old house and loading

          objects reverse or pov shots into van with B and P in shot

* dialogue if poss and B and P either directing or carrying stuff in.

In these cases shots must be MCU or tighter to let mic get close.

3) Supplementary shots

Ext: Reaction of passers by/spectators

          Trees with leaves falling in square

          View across to building site and CU of new house

          Shot list cont'd

B. New House

(NB if poss. go in removal van for pov of ride or better still go with B and P in their car
to get o/s pov and comments)

1) Emotive cutaways

Int/Ext? Look on P's face

          Look on B's face

          (Story telling moment...? When contemplating view from window – or size of

          rooms – may be good or bad, but must have pov to go with it)

Ext: View from outside mound paninto window to see B and P

Brand new front door

Int: Saxophone... where is it? (NB nice to film move of sax if not packed up)

2) Action sequences

(Min 3 shot variation again)

Ext*:   Men carrying stuff in P directing

* P and B unpacking * Cups of tea made and drunk

3) Supplementary sequences

Establishing shot of new house on building site – order among chaos

Start CU on cathedral spire – pull out to show relationship to new estate.

BIBLIOGRAPHY

Evans, Harold (1997) *Pictures on a Page: Photojournalism, Graphics and Picture Editing*. London: Pimlico.

Macdonald, Kevin & Mark Cousins (1996) *Imagining Reality/The Fable Book of Documentary*. London: Faber & Faber.

Nichols, Bill (1991) *Representing Reality*. Bloomington: Indiana University Press.

Rabiger, Michael (1998) *Directing the Documentary* (3rd edn.). Boston: Focal Press.

Warren, Charles (ed.) (1996) *Beyond Document: Essays on Non-fiction Film*. London: New England University Press.

USEFUL WEBSITES

www.documentary.org/

www.documentaryfilms.net/

www.der.org

www.scriptsearch.com

www.singlelane.com/escript/

02 **narrativity and intent in documentary production** searle kochberg

THE IMAGE

The objective nature of photography confers on it a quality of credibility absent from all other picture-making.

André Bazin, *The Ontology of the Photographic Image* (1967: 13)

The documentary mode ... call it 'real reportage' or what you will ... remains imprisoned within an historical form of the regime of truth and sense.

John Tagg, *The Burden of Representation* (1988: 102)

At the heart of documentary production is an engagement with the Real: for some the Real is what is experienced, can be objectively recorded and is tangible. For others the Real is what eludes description, defies categorisation and slips through the net. For still others it is both.

Many documentary makers would go along to a certain extent with the quote from André Bazin above: that the camera can offer a creditable window-on-reality, one that is immediate and transparent. However, most makers would also find Bazin's faith in naturalism* too simplistic today. Creative expression – unavoidable, even if you try – means subjectivity and intent*.

We need to ask questions regarding what we photograph (as opposed to what we do not), why we make particular choices, how these choices might affect the performance of our social actors on camera, and who might benefit from the 'shaping' devices we put in place? Once we begin to engage with these questions, we realise that representation* is always more that natural resemblance: it implies value judgment.

The second quote, from John Tagg, alludes to a postmodern reading of documentary, which denies any Bazin-like transparency in image-making, and at one extreme produces statements like 'there is no such thing as documentary' (Trinh T. Minh-ha in Renov 1993: 90). In the postmodern paradigm all images are caught up irredeemably in the languages of power, in the discourses of hierarchy. Hence 'real' images on our screens are best understood as naturalised – images that only look real but are instead complex constructs that are informed by the interests of the power-brokers in society.

Those who argue such a position would, however, have a hard time convincing many non-fiction makers, who continue to argue passionately for some indexical* value to their images. A case in point is the video shot by a WPVI-TV news helicopter on 13 July 2000. The Philadelphia news team captured on video the beating of Thomas Jones by city police, which revived images of the beating of Rodney King in Los Angeles by police in 1991. Clearly, video images such as these provide some visual record of events. Their literal, natural meaning is evident to anyone, even before implied, symbolic* meanings are considered. The images evidence violent police behaviour before cultural interpretations – lines of inquiry, judgments and explanations – are placed on them. Their indexical quality is undeniable and reveals, if not 'the' truth, than at least 'a' truth 'which is original and provocative' (Michael Jackson, ex-Controller of BBC2 and ex-Chief Executive of Channel 4, quoted in Macdonald & Cousins 1998: 373).

As documentary makers, we are faced with a complex set of parameters to take into account. We must steer a steady course through representation and remain alert to the bias and cultural shapings that affect our work, and that can change over time. At the same time we must remain positive to the force of non-fiction which is grounded in some version of actuality and experience.

Having spent some paragraphs arguing for the immediacy of the photographic image, what if we now consider self-conscious manipulation or expression in documentary practice? Does this contravene an ethical code of documentary? For some it does, for some it does not. Certainly for Direct Cinema* purists the integrity of an unadorned image is paramount (see below). But since expression is a precondition of any filmic process, why not use the rhetorical tools at our disposal to persuade?

Many people argue that rhetorical devices* need not be perceived as necessarily deceptive, but can work as aids in achieving 'assertions or implications about actuality' (Carl Plantinga in Bordwell & Carroll 1996: 310). As Nick Fraser argues:

> Documentaries must surely be regarded like non-fiction books or journalism – anything should go in the matter of technique, and the only real criterion for a good film is whether it tells the truth or not. (Quoted in Macdonald & Cousins 1998: 367)

Under consideration in the next section will be rhetorical styles operating in documentary practice, and the validity of Fraser's point of view. Put to the test will be the assertion that documentary can be 'openly expressive, manipulative, and rhetorical' and still fulfil its social function (see Plantinga in Bordwell & Carroll 1996: 311).

RHETORICAL STYLE

Many writers on film have studied the differing narrational styles used by documentary makers to achieve a persuasive effect in their work. Bill Nichols is perhaps the writer who has written most extensively on these rhetorical modes in documentary.[1] His categories are easy to apply for students of film and for this reason we shall use them here.

The first category of documentary we shall consider is perhaps one that we are most familiar with – the 'fly-on-the-wall' style, which Nichols calls the 'Observational' mode. Celebrated already for five decades in the existentialist writings of Bazin and the Direct Cinema makers of the 1960s/1970s, the mode is distinguished by:

- a naturalistic format based on long shots, long takes, natural light, synchronous sound, no direct address, and absence of overt expression.
- an absence of voice-over ('voice-of-god') commentary.
- an absence of interviews with 'social actors'.
- an absence of re-enactments.
- editing that emphasises 'real time' and spatial realism.
- an emphasis on loose causality.

The second category of documentary is the 'Expository' mode. This type of rhetorical style is exemplified by:

- a classic Realist format: the documentary equivalent of the classic Hollywood film.
- an authoritative, didactic voice-over commentary, 'speaking for or on behalf of someone or something' (Nichols 1991: 34).
- non sync sound and/or interviews – where witnesses' comments serve to support the film-maker's overarching arguments and do not function as arguments in their own right (Nichols 1991: 48).

- images (archive, rostrum etc) that illustrate or counterpoint the main verbal arguments (Nichols 1991: 34).
- elliptical editing, and edits which establish metaphors and lines of reasoning.

The third category is the 'Interactive' mode of documentary, which is distinguished by:

- antirealist interventions.
- the self-conscious presence of the maker.
- interactions between maker/social actors/audience.
- interviews generating debates and contradictions.
- direct address.
- juxtapositions of images and/or sounds to affect a multiplicity of viewpoints.
- testimonies and oral histories on film.

Finally, the fourth category is the 'Reflexive' mode, characterised by:

- breaks in verisimilitude* which alert audiences to the uncertainties that can inform documentary truths.
- a self-conscious use of genre conventions as a challenge to any window-on-reality.
- a self-reflection around the gathering of evidence in the documentary.
- an inclusion of self-conscious fabrication, e.g. imaginative reenactments.

The four categories should not be seen as totally discrete from one another. Often a single documentary will have features of more than one mode. However, as a starting position the categories help us think about strategies in documentary practice and the implications for meaning, as we shall explore below.

Titicut Follies (Bridgewater Film Co. Inc., 1967) is a renowned 'observational' documentary directed by Frederick Wiseman. It records conditions inside a state institution for the criminally insane, in Bridgewater, Massachusetts, and is named after the inmates' musical review, scenes of which begin and end the documentary.

Wiseman, whose contract with WNET (a PBS station) gave him creative freedom vis-à-vis subject matter and film length, has commented since the film's release that the documentary was conceived 'out of the absolute sense of shock about what Bridgewater was about' (quoted in Grant & Sloniowski 1998: 239).

At first glance, the film exemplifies the ethics of Direct Cinema, where an attempt is made to present 'uncontrolled events as faithfully as possible by using synchronous sound, no voice-over narration, and unmanipulative editing' (Allen & Gomery 1985: 215). In other words, there is a belief on Wiseman's part that the truth of his images will win out. But also on display is a self-conscious authorial intent. The film describes, yes, but it also expresses an opinion. And occasionally Wiseman creates a tension between the two in a single sequence.

At this point it is worth considering an extract from the film. Approximately 45 minutes into the film is a sequence where one of the inmates, Malinowsky, is held down by guards and force-fed by a doctor. The sequence is shot in natural light with a hand-held camera. The emaciated, naked body of Malinowsky is followed by the camera into the consulting room. There, he is laid on a bed and a lubricated pipe is forced down one of his nostrils.

The subject matter, disturbing as it is, does not alone account for the power of the sequence. This is largely achieved by the innovative tension set up by the juxtaposition of naturalistic form with expressive *mise-en-scène* and editing. Here, the accurate recording of an event is married with expressive 'choker' close shots of the inmate, the feeder-funnel, the doctor, the guards: all achieved at arms length with a zoom lens.

Halfway through the sequence, the scene is intercut with shots of the embalming of Malinowsky's body on a mortuary slab, with close shots of the face. As the sequence cuts back and forth across time and space, so the ambient, sync sound rises and falls, is evident or absent: the shots in the mortuary are totally silent. The meaning is clear: dead or alive, it makes no difference.

In this example of Direct Cinema, the descriptive, reportage style of the images is counter-balanced by a 'tactless', probing (and voyeuristic?), self-conscious form.[2] What is achieved is rhetorical strength. Naturalism and expression work together to achieve a truth which is as thought-provoking as it is disturbing.

West Indians, written by Barbadian poet George Lamming and directed by Jack Gold, is a fine example of an 'expository' documentary. It was made as an insert for the BBC current affairs programme *Tonight* in 1963, and is an interesting case study because it bears many of the hallmarks of a typical Realist broadcast documentary of those years, and yet conveys something of the voice of otherness as well.

Tonight was a long-running BBC news magazine programme (1957–65). This early evening series was famous for its lively, quirky approach to current affairs. For instance, from 1957 to 1960, actor/singer Cy Grant sang the news in Calypso! Into the programme's format were included short, non-fiction films directed by people such as Jack Gold and presented by reporters such as Alan Whicker and Fyfe Robertson. These documentary inserts were early examples of television 'vérité' production, with extensive use of lightweight, hand-held cameras, transistorised sound recorders and fast film stock. The subjects of the short films were strictly controlled by the BBC editorial team, as were their structure. The focus was very much on human interest stories.[3]

The 11-minute piece represents that moment in the representation of African-Caribbeans in British film when the theme of race-relations was the principal one explored by (white) liberal* institutions.[4] The documentary is a humanist* plea by a public broadcasting corporation for equality, freedom and the dignity of 'man'.

Realist, 'expository' documentaries rely heavily on the effacement of their own codes, and on the coherency, logic and closure of their syntax. In this documentary, the world represented is recognisable and lacking in any contradiction, and the *mise-en-scène*, editing and ambient sound do not, by and large, draw attention to themselves. The narrative is delivered clearly and logically through an overarching voice-over: we, as spectators, are guided through the film by it, and all the images are designed to illustrate perfectly Lamming's elegant prose.

An anonymous African-Caribbean male is the subject of the film. He is given no voice, and no name, like all the other black persons featured in the film. This recent 'West Indian' immigrant to the UK is differentiated only from 'English' (i.e. white) people in the film. The audience is encouraged to empathise with his plight, the prejudice he suffers, and to feel sorry for him. But, the images and sounds of black experience circa 1963 as represented here – cricket, ghettos, laundry rooms, buses, trains, hospital corridors – do little to challenge societal stereotypes.

This 'slice of life' might have benefited from allowing the subject of the film to engage in some way with the audience and film-makers through direct address or interviews. But, in a Realist film such as this, nothing must draw attention away from the overall logic of the narrative.

And yet earlier I spoke of the voice of otherness in the film. Well, Lamming's voice-over is not always just an instrument for articulating bland, liberal values, despite his BBC accent: his own identity does assert itself at times and breaks through the purely humanist agenda. For instance, near the end of the film, the voice-over suddenly drops the patronising 'victim' discourse and goes on the attack with the words, 'the politics of colour may disappear when workers recognise that their distance from the source of power is the same, their interests identical'. But moments of this kind are all too rare in the film. Any political loose ends are neatly tidied up by narrative's end with the happy sounds of a steel band and an energetic montage of previously seen images. The last shots achieve a perfect closure, and the film ends as it began with images of a cricket international: England versus the West Indies!

This publicly-funded film, designed to educate after the riots in Notting Hill and Nottingham (both in 1958), chooses to label victims rather than challenge stereotypes and engage in progressive racial politics. Hence, despite the obvious quality of the writing and the editing, the film fails to empower or activate its social actors or audiences. Ultimately, the expository format used here merely placates: it does not stimulate.

Mother Ireland is a Derry Film & Video Collective production directed by Anne Crilly in 1988. Through interview and archive material, the film debates past and present images of Irish women – real and otherwise – and the changing relevance of archetypes such as 'Mother Ireland' which, as a rallying cry for nationalists since the eighteenth century, has symbolised Ireland's subjugation and helplessness.[5]

At first glance, the film bears many of the hallmarks of the expository format: voice-over, archival footage, period songs and an overarching linear syntax. But a self-conscious partiality is immediately evident in the feminist commentary of the voice-over. And this female, Irish voice does not dominate as one would expect in the expositional* mode. Rather it acts as a link between interviews. Most of the argument is articulated through the testimonies of the many Irish women interviewed in the film, including Bernadette Devlin (politician), Sighle Humphries (activist), Margaret MacCurtain (historian), Nell McCafferty (journalist), Mairead Farrell (activist, member of IRA), Pat Murphy (film-maker) and Stephanie Peppard (housewife/mother). Of note is Sighle Humphries' testimony where the interviewer is heard out-of-frame, and the interviewee directly addresses the camera, thus acknowledging a three-way, interactive dialogue between the maker, the subject/s of the film and the audience.

Despite the narrative's trajectory from the eighteenth century to the present, the interviews affect a chequered past, not an uninterrupted shift from oppression to action. A feminist 'oral history' (Nichols 1991: 54) is constructed which is not without its contradictions. In the last 15 minutes of this 'interactive' documentary, the participants sum up the relevance of 'Mother Ireland' to them. Although the overall conclusion – reinforced by the more-or-less Realist logic of the film – is that the image today is negative and/or irrelevant, any singularity of viewpoint is avoided by the juxtaposition of varying comments, images and sounds.

This is a documentary with a difference, where there is a challenge to mainstream representation through the assertion of female identity, multiplicity and diversity. Unlike *West Indians*, which pays lip service to marginalised voices, *Mother Ireland* gives voice to Irish women who tell their own stories; in so doing, the film reveals a complexity, a truth which is original and provocative.

Another more recent interactive documentary, Eyal Sivan's *The Specialist* (Momento & Arcapix, 1999), manipulates digitally what is clearly a defining image of twentieth-century realism: Eichmann seated in his bullet-proof glass cubicle during his 1961 trial in Jerusalem. Using digital technology, the faces of those in the courtroom are now reflected subtly in the glass of the cubicle. Here sombre images of the war criminal are deliberately conflated with those of the witnesses to his crimes to expressive effect.

Sivan has stated that the film focuses on Eichmann (rather than the survivors) because of his value as a witness.[6] However, at the same time the film opens up for the spectator wider questions around window-on-reality evidence through its subtle digital interventions. By raising the issue of manipulation, the film heralds the concerns of the 'reflexive' mode of documentary. Throughout its running time, *The Specialist* presents a fascinating dialogue between authentic record and illusionism: a project akin to that of Dziga Vertov and the French New Wave film-makers.

Our last example is the documentary feature, *The Thin Blue Line* (Channel 4/American Playhouse/Program Development Company, 1988), directed by Errol Morris. In this reflexive documentary discernable breaks in verisimilitude are foregrounded to alert audiences to the uncertainties and contingencies that inform documentary evidence. The film uses the conventions of the Hollywood film noir genre – subjective flashbacks, low-key lighting, exaggerated camera angles etc. – to challenge the unarguable veracity of visual evidence and to assert a non-fiction director's freedom to dramatise.

At this point a close reading of a short extract from the film would be useful. The ten-minute sequence under review focuses on interviews with the Millers, who have

figure 4
The Thin Blue Line:
expressive lighting emphasises
the subjective nature of the
re-enactment of the murder scene

identified Randall Adams as the murderer of the policeman: it occurs approximately 47 minutes into the film.

The sequence begins with 'star witness' Mrs Miller, talking on camera about her interest in playing amateur sleuth. There follows an ironic montage of black and white images from a 1950s' television detective series featuring 'Boston Blackie' and a subjective flashback to the crime scene. Re-enactments of this scene have already punctuated the film. The self-conscious generic details of the *mise-en-scène* are therefore familiar to the viewer – a detail shot of the red light atop the policeman's car, high and low angle shots of the murder scene, low key lighting, shadows, the saturated blue hues and so on – but the Miller flashbacks promise new insights.

The Miller car is now also included in the re-enactment scene, accompanying the murderer's car and the policeman's. The first subjective flashback of Mrs Miller's comprises a low angle wide shot with the Miller car in the foreground and the two other vehicles beyond. This is followed immediately by a subjective flashback of Mr Miller's which features a detail shot of a gun and a high angle, low-key shot of the body of the policeman falling to the ground. But this point of view is clearly not Mr Miller's if we are to believe his verbal evidence: there he claims that his car has already pulled away from the immediate crime scene by the time of the shooting. There follow in this sequence repeated flashbacks to the crime scene, some of which again do not coincide with the verbal accounts of the Millers.

In film noir features it is, of course, standard practice to present as subjective flashbacks what are in fact restricted, third-person narrational views of the incidents and not the viewpoint of the characters (see for instance *Citizen Kane* (Orson Welles, 1941)). By using this convention in documentary re-enactments, however, Morris alerts us to the dramatic licence he has taken with the Millers' testimony. The repetition of the flashbacks again and again – here and throughout the film, often with minor but significant changes – awaken in the spectator a nightmarish sense of compulsive repetition and uncanny self-consciousness.

At the end of the sequence, Randall Adams' attorney repudiates Mrs Miller's evidence and calls into question the likelihood of the Millers having been at the crime scene at all that night. For the spectator, any vestige of confidence in the verisimilitude of the last ten minutes of screen time has gone. Yet, despite Morris' manipulative assault on a central project of documentary – the presentation of reliable evidence – the assault is not absolute. By the film's end, a satisfying solution to the film's central enigma, 'who done it?', is arrived at and verisimilitude is restored. For this reason, the many claims made by critics for this film as an unflinching assault on documentary truth are rather overstated. At the film's end, narrative closure and evidence win out: Randall Adams is vindicated by David Harris' admission of guilt in a taped interview.

The preceding pages make the point again and again that anything goes where documentary technique is concerned: the only real criterion is whether the film articulates a truth or not (to paraphrase Nick Fraser's comment quoted at the beginning of this chapter). Even the contrivances of *The Thin Blue Line* do little to undermine the validity of its denouement in the last scene. As practitioners we must ensure that whatever style we use, it is appropriate to the material and that it helps reveal truths that are original and provocative. In the next section, we will consider emplotment in documentary, where narrative models are influenced by modes from fiction film and television. Implications for meaning and ethics will be discussed.

NARRATIVE PATTERNING

The last section demonstrated that 'anything goes' in modes of formal expression in documentary, to the extent that today non-fiction film-makers feel confident in utilising the full gamut of choices available to fiction film-makers. Any number of different rhetorical styles can be usefully employed to convey truths, given the fact that the distinction between documentary and fiction is not based on formal differences in the first instance.

As formal styles vary in documentary so do narrative patterns. Narrative patterning is, of course, a precondition of any documentary for without it the development of a line of inquiry is impossible. However, it is quite a conceptual leap from this to the assumption made by certain commentators that you can therefore deconstruct the distinction between fiction and non-fiction.[7] For structure, theme and causality do not in themselves rule out a responsible and honest engagement with one's subject.

Nevertheless, when narrative models from popular fiction inform documentaries – as they have in recent years (examples being documentary features* and docu-soaps*) – the ethical issues of honesty and responsibility must be considered. These particular narrative models may provide documentary makers with a useful notational short hand and at the same time provide pleasure for audiences, but a responsible maker will always endeavour to ensure also that any narrative patterns correspond to 'actual ... relationships in the relevant courses of events' (Carroll in Bordwell & Carroll 1996: 289).

Returning to *The Thin Blue Line* briefly, we can see that its self-conscious narrational motifs* – non-linear structure, confused causality, unclear motivations, narrational blind alleys, fatalism, and unattractive characters – all parallel the real life miasma of confused events documented by the maker. In the case studies that follow, what will be of ultimate interest to us is the extent to which the emplotment devices affect more than just a narrative logic or pleasure, and actually help to illuminate provocative truths.

When We Were Kings (Polygram/DAS, 1996) is a documentary feature directed by Leon Gast. Documentary features like this one are marked by mainstream (fiction) film influences that play a part in the shaping of the subject matter. The film – which documents the famous 'Rumble in the Jungle' bout between Mohammed Ali and

George Foreman in Zaire in 1974 – follows the archetypal structure of a Hollywood adventure film, itself a manifestion of Vladimir Propp's folk tale model.[8] This takes the form of an action-packed narrative where a hero, motivated by a lack or insufficiency in something, departs on a journey where he engages in a contest with a villain, defeats him and returns in glory. The plot structure is made up of a finite set of single actions or 'functions', so called because of the function they serve in the development of the plot.

The post-production history of this documentary makes only too evident how actuality footage is included or excluded, shaped and reshaped, when constraints are brought to bear on it. The original concept of the documentary for which independent film-maker, Leon Gast, was hired highlighted the concert (featuring James Brown, B. B. King and Miriam Makeba) which accompanied the fight. Unfortunately for Gast, legal and financial problems held up the project for years. What emerged after an incredible 22 years was the current structure which foregrounds the heroic odyssey of Ali – in search of his African roots – and his regaining of the heavyweight 'crown'.

A rather facile, linear rendition of the Zaire event has emerged which precludes an in-depth examination of the identity politics surrounding it. Themes that are thrown up – such as imperialism versus separatism, Black versus White, dominance versus subservience, and idealism versus reality – are marginalised in the rush to tell a rattlingly good tale not dissimilar to the *Rocky* movies (1976, 1979, 1982, 1985, 1990).

In its present format, this expository documentary cannot really do justice to the complexities hinted at in the narrative themes. What emerges is a fast-paced entertainment around myth-making and star personalities.

Another documentary feature, *One Day in September* (Arthur Cohn/Passion Pictures, 1999) enjoyed a 'multiple' theatrical run* in the UK recently and was screened as part of the *Storyville* series on BBC2. The film, directed by Kevin Macdonald, takes as its central focus the 21-hour hostage crisis at the 1972 Munich Olympics when Palestinians held Israeli athletes captive.

figure 5
**When We Were Kings:
Mohammed Ali as hero of
a documentary charting
his return to glory**

As in our previous example, narrative drive is given priority in a structure designed to engage a theatrical audience. The film largely adopts a linear, expository format, with the narrative sticking closely to the chronology of events on 5 September 1972. The story is told in a punchy style through a mix of voice-over, moving and still image archive footage, interviews and reenactments.

Generic influences from fiction film are evident in the shaping of the narrative as well. But as in the previous example, their inclusion is not not intended to challenge the veracity of the evidence presented (as in the case of *The Thin Blue Line*), but rather to add to the film's verisimilitude. The film's 'treatment' takes the form of a heroic tragedy where 11 Israeli team members are victims of the terrible state of division that exists between Israelis and Palestinians. Its much-promoted 'documentary thriller' format also ensures that suspense is maintained throughout, by restricting the spectator's knowledge of the events to scenes as they unravel in the story.

This generic treatment of events, however, also reduces complex issues to fit the format, something for which the film has been much criticised. The Palestinian writer, Edward Said (2000), has been particularly damning of the film because of its lack of an adequate Palestinian perspective. Macdonald, in turn, has answered the accusations by arguing that the story of the hostage crisis 'naturally ... provoke[s] sympathy for the Israeli athletes. To make [the film] any other way would be perverse' (quoted in Macnab 2000: 11).

Many important questions raised by the film go unanswered in an attempt to maintain narrative drive, such as the relationship between the 'Black September' group and the PLO, and the degree of East German involvement in the hostage-taking. If one is never in any doubt of the film's excitement and suspense, it is true to say that one might have expected a more complex historical commentary thirty years on.

Like the previous example, this documentary feature is very engaging, but there is a warning for makers to be heeded here as well. In seeking wider audiences for our work, we documentary makers need to ensure that we maintain a complexity and a level of debate in our engagement with truths, something hard to bring off in a slavish tracking of generic conventions.

Shown as part of the *Cutting Edge* series on Channel 4, Paul Watson's *A Wedding in the Family* (United Productions, 2000) is a further example of a feature length documentary – this time made for television – which incorporates themes evident in popular fiction forms. An early exponent of the docu-soap in his productions such as *The Family* (1974) and *Sylvania Waters* (1993), Watson has recently turned to 'the core establishment of middle England' (Collins 2000: 9) for his subjects.

Focusing as it does on community, marriage, family etc., *A Wedding in the Family* could so easily have fallen victim to the 'soft and bubbly' approach evident in recent lightweight docu-soaps.[9] However, in the hands of Watson, the film does not so much celebrate rites of integration as question them. It mobilises a non-linear*, associative editing* style establishing metaphorical relationships to dissect the minutiae of activities and responses of the social actors involved. A convincingly open-ended look at middle-England values is arrived at through the complex weave of interrelated themes such as male versus female, public versus private, and continuity versus discontinuity.

Paul Watson, interviewing off camera, interacts with his subjects sensitively to allow them 'space' to reflect on the 'rocks under the surface' of marriage (quoted in Collins 2000: 9). In the process, two of the family members emerge as the protagonists of the film: Sue and Steve, the stepmother and father of the bride. Sue's interviews encapsulate the tragic resignation of a woman locked unhappily into the traditional structures of marriage, whilst Steve's fragmented statements to camera reveal a striving for recognition, power and authority in the public sphere.

If, at times, the candid nature of Sue's comments makes one anxious about how informed her consent actually was, and if the male/female division around sacrifice versus power seems overplayed at times, these are the only reservations I have about this film. Overall, the narrative patterning offers a provocative view of a subject which so often is treated in a purely celebratory tone (as with romantic comedy), with none of the irony, pain and loss evident here.

The British version of *Big Brother* (Bazal Productions for Channel 4, 2000, 2001, 2002), like the previous example, features a 'family' of characters and is preoccupied with socio-sexual mores. But here the similarity ends. This series in its first season attracted much comment in the press, a lot of it negative – particularly in relation to its 'soft' approach to documentary.[10] And on one level the programme is indeed a celebration of vacuity. For even by the conventions of the average docu-soap, at times the unchanging domestic arena, the mundane continuing stories and the paucity of dramatic incident hardly seem to justify the air time afforded the series.[11] This is in spite of the fact that the ten social actors were chosen for their abilities to perform on camera, to be articulate, to be individual, to be funny, and to be part of a team.[12]

However, added narrative value is to be had in the game-show format, with the social actors doubling as contestants in this actuality entertainment. The mantra of the cast members throughout – 'it's only a game-show' – reflects the Proppian logic at play here, where the group of protagonists battle it out in a (domestic) arena, defeat the villain ('Nasty Nick'), and where one of them (Craig) goes on to win the prize at the end of the nine weeks.

Big Brother represents the first fully integrated 'parallel programme' (web + television) experience in the UK, where a programme is designed to be seen both on a new media platform – in this case the 24/7 £5 million *Big Brother* website – and on a terrestrial channel. Ultimately, the series is of interest to makers of programming because of the pleasures afforded the 'viewser' (viewer-cum-PC user) through its intertextual* – multimedia, multigenre – approach. This multimedia event combines a TV lean-back experience with an IT lean-forward experience, with its target audience adding impetus to the narrative through emails to producers, website-hits, and viewer-to-viewer running commentaries by (mobile) phone on the live webcasts.[13]

In the new-media environment of today, one must expect (and encourage) approaches to media product that challenge old boundaries. And as a new technological/conceptual departure for Reality TV*, *Big Brother* deserves our praise. What needs to be ensured, however, is that its success does not jeopardise the commissioning of more solid, less 'soft' factual programming in the future, as some media commentators have feared.

Narrative patterning in documentary does not, in itself, mean that the work is a deceitful manipulation. Patterning – when used with ethical rigour – allows makers to shape material into subjective truths that illuminate and stimulate debate. The fact that narrative models are not always mobilised to this end does not in itself make the excercise an erroneous one from the start. Any line of inquiry will always benefit from a structure that is provoking to the spectator, and is appropriate to the themes and issues at hand.

AUTHORSHIP

It has been my position throughout this chapter that narrativity and formal expression do not necessarily undermine the project of documentary. In the right hands, these elements help organise and articulate rigorous truths.

Given Bazin's commitment to the objectivity of the photographic image, it is rather ironic that he and fellow contributors at *Cahiers du Cinéma* in the 1950s should also have been responsible for the promotion of authorship in film.[14] In their polemical essays, a director is identified as an *auteur** if he/she stamps a personal – i.e. subjective – style on the work through repeated themes and/or visual style evident from film to film.

In this final section we consider explicitly the issue of authorship in documentary practice, which we have tended to skim over in the previous sections. For despite a Bazin position adopted by many makers of documentary – self-effacement – some practitioners have a recognisable aesthetic voice in their work, where truths are mediated through their artistic obsessions in film after film.

Authorial presence is evident across the full spectrum of rhetorical styles. Consider, for instance, the table below:

Director	Documentary Title	Rhetorical Style
Jean Rouch	*Chronicle of a Summer* (1961)	interactive
Frederick Wiseman	*Titicut Follies* (1967)	observational
Orson Welles	*F For Fake* (1975)	interactive/reflexive
Molly Dineen	*Heart of the Angel* (1989)	interactive
Ken Burns	*The Civil War* (1990)	expository
Nicholas Barker	*Unmade Beds* (1997)	reflexive

In the five decades since the *Cahiers* polemic was proposed, various models have been put forward for authorship (see Cook 1985). Early models tend to focus on expressive intent, whereas more recent models also emphasise wider cultural patternings and audience interactions in the process of creating meaning. It is this latter, more inclusive model of authorship that will inform the comments below on Orson Welles' *F For Fake* (Astrophore/Saci/Janus, 1975) and Nicholas Barker's *Unmade Beds* (Chelsea Pictures, 1997).

Orson Welles carries the label of *enfant terrible* of American Cinema, because he is identified as *the* breaker of rules who could not fit into the Hollywood system adequately. And yet he is responsible for what many regard as the system's greatest film, *Citizen Kane*.

Welles' status as *auteur* is evident from the reverence afforded him by critics from Bazin (1978) onwards. In *F For Fake*, the dialectic of high versus low culture is in evidence, as it is throughout Welles' work. Here the world of fine art is counterpoised with that of fakes and copies. If the film is marked by an expressive, high cultural form – in this case self-conscious, fragmented decoupage,[15] freeze-frame, zoom and dramatic illusion, all akin to French New Wave – it also uses mainstream, low cultural thematic and visual strategies. Here, for instance, are Hollywood genre conventions – the 'great-man' biopic (the subjects being Elmyr de Hory, Clifford Irving and Welles himself) – and classic Hollywood montage.

In the early twenty-first century, with the benefit of hindsight, one can interpret the patterning of high versus low in Welles' interactive/reflexive documentary as a marker

figure 6
**F for Fake:
dramatic illusion and magic
mark Orson Welles' foray
into interactive/reflexive
documentary**

of his career history, epitomised by the interaction of European and American film styles and production contexts.

The contemporary UK documentary-maker Nicholas Barker also has an identifiable authorial style. His film, *Unmade Beds* (screened as part of the *Modern Times* series on BBC2 in 1999) is marked by a *mise-en-scène* which, along with much art-cultural product of the 1990s, demonstrates a propensity for pastiche of earlier aesthetic styles, some from film, some not.

The opening scene, as New Yorkers wake up, is a deliberate reference to *Rear Window* (Alfred Hitchcock, 1954) with its voyeuristic examination in long-shot of people through their apartment windows. The shots make the lives of the inhabitants distant and remote to the viewer, but at the same time safe to gaze at. This visual style is itself evocative of the 1930s and 1940s paintings of Edward Hopper which capture the urban alienation and isolation of anonymous individuals, seen through the windows of their dwellings.

Elsewhere in *Unmade Beds*, the 'frozen' tableaux of the social actors seen directly addressing the camera on their home turf are borrowed from Barker's earlier documentary series, *Signs of the Times* (1992). These alienating long takes evoke a modernist strategy evident in the 1960s work of Jean Luc Godard – for example, *Weekend* (1967) – itself an interpretation of the 'epic theatre' aesthetic of Bertholt Brecht.

Such is the self-evident constructedness in the production – pastiche*, 'frozen' tableau shots, episodic narrative – that the viewer is bound to question the degree of transparency that informs this documentary evidence. This is compounded by the fact that the social actors perform their stories from 'distilled' transcripts (made from earlier recorded encounters with the director (see Bruzzi 2000)), often resulting in larger-than-life performances such as Brenda's bride-to-be 'act' at the end of the film.[16]

From an early twenty-first century perspective, Barker's reflexive style can be seen as epitomised by conscious (and unconscious?) borrowings of networks of images derived from popular to fine art. Even if one is left wondering ultimately what is myth and what is reality in *Unmade Beds*, the pastiche offers a superb dramatic staging through which to represent urban alienation and different gender, ethnic and class identities.

If it is useful and appropriate at times to ascribe authorship to individual directors in documentary work, often it is not. For most documentaries are shaped by a network of forces, and not just the director's vision. In the UK programme-making context, for instance, money for productions is accessed through funding bodies such as terrestrial television channels who organise the commissioning of documentaries through individual documentary series on their channels. As witnessed in the earlier case study of *West Indians*, made for the *Tonight* programme on the BBC in the 1960s, each series has its own editorial remit. As a maker of programming you need to ensure that you develop ideas based upon the specific interests of the series' editors. Thus we can talk about a *Despatches* (Channel 4) style, a *Storyville* (BBC) style and so on, with each series differentiating its product from others to give it an identity in the marketplace.[17]

Independent writer/director/producer teams always work to a series editor's brief and their ability to attract development money and production money* from television companies will depend on their particular knowledge and slant (treatment) on the subject they wish to make a programme on, and of course on their previous track record. In today's 'tight' and competitive marketplace, terrestrial, cable, satellite and new-media programming is inevitably the product of 'pack-of-cards' financing, where several co-funding bodies are involved in a programme's making and where each source of funding is dependent on the participation of the others.

In conclusion, then, we can say that the intent of the maker plays an important part in the generation of meaning. If this were not the case, we practitioners might lose the imperative to make programmes altogether. However, ethics and rigour on our part do not alone create substantial and meaningful documentaries. As makers we need to have an appreciation of how particular production and viewing contexts also affect the meaning of our work.

As commissioning bodies shape the nature of non-fiction programming through the mobilisation of preferred styles and formats, so audiences bring to their viewing particular ethical (i.e. class/gender/sexual/cultural) frameworks which can substantially affect the 'preferred reading' – or original intent – of our work.

NOTES

1 See 'Documentary Modes of Representation', in Nichols' *Representing Reality*, 32–75.

2 See Bill Nichols' comments on Wiseman's 'tactless' style, with its disregard for 'the ideological contraints of politeness'. In *Ideology and the Image* he interprets the style as largely progressive, voyeurism notwithstanding (Nichols 1981: 209).

3 See Madden & Wilson 1974: 134–7.

4 For an equivalent in feature film, see *Flame in the Streets* (1961), written by Ted Willis and directed by Roy Baker.

5 The film bears many similarities to *The Life & Times of Rosie the Riveter*, directed by Connie Fields in 1980.

6 In an article on the film by Charlotte O'Sullivan in *The Independent*, 3 March 2000, 12, Sivan clearly supports the veracity of Eichmann's testimony. He is quoted as saying: 'I was right to focus on the perpetrator. Because he's talking from inside the system, Eichmann's testimony is a hundred times more powerful than any survivor's.'

7 For an example of this line of reasoning see Michael Renov's 'Introduction: The Truth about Non-Fiction', in Renov 1993: 1–11.

8 In the 1920s Vladimir Propp had proposed a model to define the generic structure of the Russian folk tale. For full details of his analysis, see Propp 1990.

9 Paraphrasing Mark Fiedler, ex-producer at the BBC, and quoted in Bruzzi 2000: 79.

10 See, for example, Steel 2000: 5.

11 Weekly output included: 2 x live half-hour shows; 1 x one-hour documentary; 1 x one-hour omnibus edition; 3 x half-hour shows; 24-hour web-cast on the *Big Brother* website. For details see Ritchie 2000: 9–10.

12 See Ritchie 2000: 26.

13 The second UK series of *Big Brother* (2001) added text messaging (to mobile phones) to the multimedia 'pool' in order to alert fans of any 'major' happenings in the house as soon as they occured.

14 See Bazin 'On the politique des auteurs', reprinted in Hillier 1985: 248–59.

15 Which replaces the more typical deep-focus/long take expression in Welles' fiction narratives.

16 Such are the aesthetic results that test audiences at the time of the film's release were 'convinced they were watching highly naturalistic fiction'. See Bruzzi 2000: 158.

17 There is recent evidence, however, that Channel 4 is moving away from a policy of specific content associated with specific series.

BIBLIOGRAPHY

Allen, R. & D. Gomery (1985) *Film History Theory & Practice.* New York: Newbery Award Records.

Bazin, A. (1967) *What is Cinema?* Berkeley & LA: University of California Press.

____ (1978) *Orson Welles: A Critical View.* London: Elm Tree.

Bordwell, D. & N. Carroll (eds) (1996) *Post-Theory.* London: University of Wisconsin Press.

Bruzzi, S. (2000) *New Documentary: A Critical Introduction.* London: Routledge.

Collins, M. (2000) 'The camera never lies', The Friday Review, *The Independent*, 24 March, 9.

Cook, P. (1985) (ed.) *The Cinema Book.* London: BFI.

Dovey, J. (2000) *Freakshow: First Person Media and Factual Television.* London: Pluto Press.

Grant, B. K. & J. Sloniowski (eds) (1998) *Documenting the Documentary.* Detroit: Wayne State University Press.

Hillier, J. (ed.) (1985) *Cahiers du Cinéma vol.1: The 1950s.* London: BFI/Routledge & Kegan Paul.

Macdonald, K. & M. Cousins (1998) *Imagining Reality.* London: Faber & Faber.

Macnab, G. (2000) 'Munich: the truth behind the cover-up', in The Friday Review, *The Independent*, 31 March, 11.

Madden, P. & D. Wilson (1974) 'Getting in Close', *Sight and Sound*, 43, 3, Summer, 134–7.

Nichols, B. (1981) *Ideology and the Image.* Bloomington: Indiana University Press.

_____ (1991) *Representing Reality.* Bloomington: Indiana University Press.

_____ (1994) *Blurred Boundaries.* Bloomington: Indiana University Press.

O'Sullivan, C. (2000) 'The human death merchant', The Friday Review, *The Independent*, 3 March, 12.

Propp, V. (1990) *Morphology of a Folktale.* Austin, Texas: University of Texas.

Renov, M. (ed.) (1993) *Theorising Documentary.* London: Routledge.

Ritchie, J. (2000) *Big Brother.* London: Channel 4 Books.

Said, E. (2000) 'Losers in the games', Saturday Review, *The Guardian*, 20 May, 1–2.

Steel, M. (2000) 'So when is Mad Dog going to join Big Brother?', The Thursday Review, *The Independent*, 31 August, 8.

Tagg, J. (1988) *The Burden of Representation.* London: Macmillan.

FURTHER READING

Reisz, K. & G. Millar (1968) *The Technique of Film Editing* (2nd edn.). London: Focal Press.

Rosenthal, A. (ed.) (1988) *New Challenges for Documentary*. London: University of California Press.

____ (1996) *Writing, Directing, and Producing Documentary Films and Videos*. Carbondale & Edwardsville. Southern Illinois University Press.

Rothman, W. (1997) *Documentary Film Classics*. New York: Cambridge University Press.

Williams, C. (ed.) (1980) *Realism and the Cinema*. London: Routledge & Kegan Paul.

USEFUL WEBSITES

General information on documentary content:

www.poll.imdb.com/sections/genres/documentary/

www.dmoz.org/arts/movies/film-making/documentary/

Online bibliography:

www.lib.berkeley.edu/mrc/documentarybib.html

Online sourcing of videos:

www.moviem.co.uk

Specific information on films/makers:

Titicut Follies: www.24framespersecond.com/offcamera/writings/wiseman.html

The Specialist: www.wjff.org/specialist.htm

The Thin Blue Line: www.errolmorris.com/static/film/thinblueline/

When We Were Kings: www.filmeducation.org/secondary/documentary/
    wwwkings/

One Day in September: www.filmeducation.org/secondary/documentary/
    september/

A Wedding in the Family: www.film.kopec.com/pdf/watson.pdf

Big Brother: www.bigbrotherwebsite.com/

F For Fake: www.combustiblecelluloid.com/fforfake.shtm

Unmade Beds: www.boardsmag.com/articles/online/20000316/barker.htm.

03 **audiences and documentary** marie womack

APPROACHES TO THE CONCEPT OF DOCUMENTARY AUDIENCES

No media product is made without a specific idea of the target audience, that is, who is going to watch it. Hence the notion of audience is at the centre of all media study. The discussions that follow on documentary programming are based upon the interaction between the contemporary documentary, 'high-' and 'low-brow' culture, and audiences.

In Western industrialised societies culture is categorised in various ways. We speak of 'high' and 'low' cultural taste, and of 'elite' and 'pop' culture. These categories have material effects in terms of policies and practices which shape cultures. But cultural reception of the same documentary varies according to the particular cultural context. The basic approach to exploring and attempting to understand the concept of audiences could be based on empirical research of audience or on theoretical insights (which tend to be more about the concept of audience, and also about the concept of construction of audiences). Most approaches tend to use both, research and theory, to test their ideas.

The early to mid-twentieth century saw the development of a mass culture industry which was criticised by the Frankfurt School for its threat to quality. The notions of restricted quantity, authorship, creativity and high quality were attached to a 'high brow' and that of mass quantity, lack of originality and low quality to a 'low brow'.

Audiences experience pleasure (and desire) in watching documentaries, and this pleasure is extended to certain active forms of audience participation. Currently audiences occupy changing positions of participation due to the advent of the Internet, digital technology and of 'home video' footage used en masse in docu-entertainment programmes such as *You've Been Framed* (Granada Television) and *Big Brother* (Bazal Productions for Channel 4).

In a contemporary context, John Grierson's definition of documentary as 'the creative treatment of actuality' needs to be revisited, since the current debate, centred on documentary's relationship to truth, naturalism, ethics, and subject positioning, includes contemporary interaction between the documentary maker and audience.

Debates around spectatorship have now shifted from the traditional fixed position of passivity, towards an altered position of an audience that receives, produces, participates, receives and makes new meanings. The ideology of the image, or Roland Barthes' mythology of the image, is appropriated and modified through *jouissance* into significations actively shaped by the members of audience who watch documentaries. Barthes' concept of *audience jouissance* (1977: 164) postulates that audiences partly determine for themselves pleasurable meanings which do not always comply with 'preferred readings'.

Big Brother (UK series #1, 2000) offers a self-conscious mass-audience interaction, which is visible and is likely to grow into 'openness and widening participation'. *Big Brother*'s audiences are known: they are young (20–35), in employment, single (including post-divorce), with a good level of education and with access to new technologies,[1] and their responses through their weekly vote on who is eliminated from the show demonstrate that the current debate focused around audience response and differentiation is on the right track.

AUDIENCE RESEARCH: DOCUMENTARY AS COMMODITY, AS FORM OF SOCIAL COMMUNICATION AND AS CULTURAL RESPONSE

Documentary as a media product is a commodity, intended to be sold for audience consumption, but it is also a text, having a duality in its purpose. The production of meanings is prescribed to an extent within the limitations set by the documentary itself and its producer. But these meanings are also mediated by viewers since people will get different meanings from the same documentary.

The construction of meaning, mediated through institutions, is a very complex one (see O'Sullivan *et al.* 1994: 152). Many possible alternative meanings are possible in a documentary. But some theorists warn that polysemy, or many meanings, must not be confused with pluralism (O'Sullivan *et al.* 1994: 152; 230–1). In other words spectators may contribute to making their own meanings, but that does not give them power over what documentaries are commissioned, produced and distributed.

David Morley's *Nationwide Audience*, now a classic, was a breakthrough in the 1980s. His research attempted to understand how meanings are experienced by audiences in a family or social group environment and how these meanings are then formulated so they can be shared by other members of the group. Before *Nationwide*, audience research would stress either the importance of production or of reception, but did not project an integrated perspective to this complex process.

Models of audience classification

We need to think about television as embedded in the multiple discourses of everyday life. And we need to understand what those discourses are, how they are themselves determined, how they interweave and, most crucially, how they are to be distinguished in terms of their influence relative to each other. This task of description and analysis requires both theoretical and empirical attention (Silverstone 1994: ix).

In a media sense, a whole range of discourses – languages of authority, of sport, of earning, of consuming, of caring, of domestic scene – all inform spectatorship. Discourses are a part of everyday living and form a set of complex patterns of differing spectatorships.

In the past traditional demographics were used, which are still used today. Audience profiling by social class is based on earning power or level of income: A – upper middle class; B – middle class; C1 – lower middle class; C2 – skilled working class; D – working class; and E – lowest subsistence levels.

This type of classification is based on Marx's theory of social class. The emphasis is on social subjects and their class struggle: the 'haves' – the bourgeoisie and petite bourgeoisie who possess considerable and small property and means of production, and the 'have-nots' – the proletariat, without property and without means of production. To survive the proletariat have to sell their work (intellectual, physical, and artistic) on the labour markets.

Since the 1960s the material ease and influence of the working classes has increased through a mixture of technological and communication developments which have become widely available in the marketplace, so that 'people power' has increased through consumption. Yet society still remains dominated by groups who have more access to the means of production and to the acquisition of property.

In the last two decades, Marxist theory has lost some of its influence, however, and other theoretical approaches around audience profiling have become more prevalent. One of them is based on liberal pluralism, which allows a 'pick and mix' of audience classification, traditional demographics and psychological profiling, lifestyle and attitude, expectation and taste trends. These approaches collectively take into account universal human needs (see Maslow 1970).

A pluralist notion of taste and competence is described by Pierre Bourdieu. In Bourdieu's writings on popular and high culture (and their audiences), the notions of 'pure' or aesthetic gaze and 'naïve' or popular aesthetic gaze are understood within the category of 'taste'. His oft-quoted statement is: 'Taste classifies, and it classifies the classifier' (1984: 7).

Bourdieu identifies various forms of 'capital': economic (financial resources), cultural (taste, preferences, education and knowledge), social (networks, connections, group memberships, family background), and symbolic (what is achieved when the previous three forms are recognised as legitimate and institutionalised) (see Seiter 1999: 24–6). Audiences exercise influence and power according to their access to 'capital'. Thus a division between dominant or official culture and popular culture is perpetuated. According to Bourdieu, social group A – the upper middle class (high professional, administrative and managerial) has very high financial and social capital, but not necessarily as high cultural capital. For instance, some members of group A do not necessarily have a very high educational capital because they do not need to earn their living on the labour markets.

Two groups, C1 and C2, are considered to be the 'backbone' of society and they represent the majority of the economically active population. They may have higher educational and cultural capital than their disposable income (see Hartley 1994: 70). This means they could be a part of an elitist audience so that a documentary on the Tate Gallery's Turner Prize would be within their cultural competence, despite their income level.

Group E could be either quite 'rich' or 'poor' in all but financial capital, which is at the level of subsistence. They could have a refined, connoisseur's taste, they could watch high- and middle-brow documentaries, but advertising on commercial television would not target them, since their spending power is so low.

Audiences for documentary have to be competent in the subject matter, or have an interest in what they view as their sphere of competence, to be engaged with the material adequately. The broad, mass audience (5–7 million) for *Big Brother* for instance, feels competent with the subject matter – domestic situations, game-shows and IT. Hence, when the 'Nasty Nick' revelations were at their peak, 'the *Big Brother* phenomenon achieved a huge degree of resonance, like a coaxial cable rigged-up between high and low culture'.[2]

Audience research in practice: viewing figures and audience profiling

Viewing figures of documentaries are carefully monitored by their producers and different agencies specialised in the research of social and cultural trends.

Viewing figures or television audience measurement in the 1990s was calculated with 'people meters': electronic gadgetry was wired into television sets, videos and decoders to transmit daily through telephone lines who has been watching what, when and with whom. This is now an established audience research practice in the Western industrialised world. In the UK this kind of audience measurement is supervised by the Broadcasters Audience Research Board (BARB).

When researching documentary audiences, researchers have certain parameters to observe such as ensuring that the groups are representative of the whole country as attitudes to programmes vary considerably across the UK (see Briggs & Cobley 1998).

Documentaries are commissioned and made according to audience interest and the aesthetic policies of television companies, as well as other influences such as the economic, social and political climates of the day. Their success is measured by advertising revenue in commercial television, and by audience levels and gratification in state-owned television. Programme makers and commercial interests look at television ratings, audience share and reach, before commissioning new documentaries or maintaining the existing slots for programmes.

Knowing the documentary viewing figures is useful to the managers of different television channels, but to achieve a more dynamic picture of audiences many companies use a technique (not exclusively in the UK, but used in continental Europe and the USA as well) known as 'lifestyle' profiling, which takes into account the psychological profile of the consumer, combined with their purchasing profile in the market place. This is in addition to taking account of the social class as a guide for marketing the documentary.

The French *Centre de la Communication Avancée* (CCA) established the first encyclopaedia of European lifestyles based upon 24,000 interviews in 16 European countries with a wide range of people's psychological profiles. This kind of measuring and assessing of audience is now an established practice.

Since the early 1990s, the fragmentation of television audiences has been steadily increasing, which has caused a falling off of viewing figures for popular shows. Audience figures for Saturday night programmes such as *Blind Date* and *Big Break* have fallen fast – by 30 and 49 per cent respectively – in the last six years. Currently, docu-soaps attract a mass audience, but since there are many more channels than before the introduction of cable and satellite television in the early 1990s, audiences are diluted and it is only a matter of time before popular terrestrial telecasts lose their grip on audience share.

Target audiences and Big Brother

The interaction between audiences and programming is more elaborate now. As a result, audiences occupy a different position now, brought on by the digital revolution and the internet (integral to docu-soaps such as *Ibiza Uncovered* (Sky One, 1998) and *Big Brother*).

Big Brother's target audience was clear to Channel 4 and to advertisers who placed their ads during *Big Brother*'s air time. Yet here is an example where the concrete boundaries of target audience were challenged. B and C1 audiences were consuming what, in a less interactive text, would have been product designed primarily for C2–E audiences.

By watching documentaries such as *Big Brother,* spectators plug into a kind of imaginary 'ready-made' community, and experience pleasure and desires. Recent technological developments in web-casting extend this pleasure into certain active forms of audience participation. For instance, at the time of 'Nasty Nick's' departure from the house in the first series (2000), many viewers notified each other via email and mobile telephones to tune in 'live' on the Web, so as to watch and discuss events as they were happening and evolving. All national newspapers reported on Nick's fall from grace in *Big Brother,* and *The Sun* even picked up the story of 'Nasty Nick' Bateman's departure as a headline sensation.

Big Brother employs other interactive textual devices and strategies, such as direct address, which takes the form of a 'confessional' interview in an isolated room away from other participants. While watching the 'confessional' the spectator may or may not be persuaded by the participant, and this feeds into how she/he will vote (or not).

Thus, in conclusion, the shift in the construction of documentary audiences has now moved from more traditional fixed positions of subjectivity, towards a new altered position of a more interactive subjectivity.

DOCUMENTARY AS MEDIATED DISCOURSE: HIGH-, MIDDLE- AND LOW-BROW AESTHETICS AND SPECTATORSHIP

Case study: Arena as 'high-brow' mediated discourse

'I hope I can move people and change the world.'
Derek Jarman, in *Arena – Derek Jarman: A Portrait* (BBC, 1991)

This 60-minute documentary film was produced and directed by Mark Kidel in 1991 for the BBC. Derek Jarman died of AIDS while still in his prime: in 1991 he was already diagnosed HIV positive. He was a multi-talented artist who painted, made films, and loved gardening.[3] In the film, he looks at peace with himself and smiles often.

Jarman walks through rooms which are reminiscent of exhibition spaces: he stops from time to time, touches an object, gazes through the window and talks earnestly about his personal history. Before he looks at a family photo album, 8mm colour film footage of Jarman's childhood shows him and his baby sister in a garden paddling pool splashing water with their feet. They giggle and are obviously aware of the camera but take to it graciously. These children in their golden years are shown in a colourful summer garden and on the beach, playing ball with their mother.

Then Jarman shows a few photographs from an album. He was close to both parents and his baby sister. But his father became 'a bit monstrous, force-fed me when I did not eat and threw me through the window ... and my mother, ah, well, she loved him and stood by looking at it helplessly'.

Jarman tenderly touches an indoor ornamental tree, given to him by a neighbour in 1963. He says, 'If this plant could talk it could tell you all you want to know about me.' He mentions that in 1964 he went 'wild' and went to Greece, slept outdoors in the ruins of temples and met his first lover.

The content of this documentary is about an extraordinary artist juxtaposed with the past images of an ordinary existence. This multi-talented artist tried to change the world and pushed forward the tradition of poetry, liberation and surrealism in his personal dream images. The style of the documentary conforms to Jarman's style of being: of lightness, of elegance, with a poetic, almost lyrical, sense, and an allusion to the wildness and anger which hides sensitivity and deep feelings.

The aesthetic codes are complex and therefore designed for a selected, high-brow cultural elite. They refer to a refined cultural capital, with knowledge of ancient Greece, of abstraction, of beauty, of European religious paintings, of symbols of crucifixion, of pure energy, of pure vision, of Shakespearian inspiration, of Surrealism. In terms of social class the programme addresses the upper and middle classes.

Case study: Wildlife on One as 'middle-brow' mediated discourse

This BBC Natural History Unit production is yet another tour de force for David Attenborough, the director/presenter, and Mike Salisbury, its producer. One exemplary programme, *The Secret Life of Plants: Growing* (TBS Productions and BBC, 1995), focuses on the South American rain forest. The subject of the documentary is an extraordinary plant whose sack of seeds falls from the top of a tree down to the forest floor, then releasing thousands of seed. Then tiny shoots appear, sense the light and then spread as far as six feet to find a vertical surface on which they can attach. If they do not find it they starve and die. The time-lapse photography captures the plant growing upwards, first with small, circular leaves and then with bigger leaves through which it produces food for itself.

Many months later, and fifty feet above the forest floor, the 'cheese plant' reaches its maturity at the top of the forest canopy. Soon it will produce a sack of new seeds and the same life cycle will renew itself.

The contents of the documentary concentrates on the cheese plant, its surroundings, and its life cycle. Attenborough's voice is added in the form of voice-over, and a music track intervenes occasionally in solemn tones.

The style is naturalistic: real location and real plants are used, with the help of time-lapse photography. There are close-ups of the plants and the rain forest canopy, where leaves are intricately and perfectly choreographed in a kind of chlorophyll slow dance. A canopy of leaves blocks out the sky as seen from the forest floor. They all need light, water and a few minerals from the soil to make food, such as sugar and starches for themselves.

The aesthetic codes are easily decoded, because the imagery and vocabulary are close enough to everyday living. The programme addresses 'general' audiences with more cultural and social capital, and perhaps less economic and symbolic capital, or the 'middle-brow' audience. This constitutes the great majority of the population, whose keen interest in nature documentaries is reflected in the programme's mass audiences.

Case study: Best of Ibiza Uncovered as 'low-brow' mediated discourse

'In the future everyone will be world famous for fifteen minutes.'
Andy Warhol

In 1997 a small Sky One production crew began to make a fly-on-the-wall documentary about life on the island of Ibiza, just 17 miles off the coast of Spain. Some of the first participants, Louise Hudson and Sarah Watson from Rotherham, soon became minor celebrities in the tabloid press, with their sensational account in the documentary of having sex with forty men between the two of them in a two-week holiday. The show seemingly offers a glimpse of a hedonistic world in the sun, where anything goes: sex, bare flesh on the beaches, drinks, drugs, gigantic parties – an escape from the reality back home.

A notable sequence of *Best of Ibiza Uncovered* is one of the 'Manumission club' brothers, who had a small Manchester club before establishing themselves as the biggest weekly party in the world. Eight thousand people go to watch the Manumission club's outrageous floor shows. It seems that *Ibiza Uncovered* helped the brothers Mike and Andy to such an extent that they also opened a Manumission restaurant, hotel bar and travel company. The sequence focuses on Andy, who looks after the business. He is seen walking outside the venue checking the hedonist revellers' behaviour. The clubbers are all young and look wide awake in spite of the early hours of the morning. After a 'dissolve' Andy faces the camera with his female companion. He is businesslike and says: 'When will *Ibiza Uncovered* finally die? It's UNSTOPPABLE!'

The style is fly-on-the-wall with natural locations, and the hedonistic holidaymakers are all in a fun-frenzied party mood. It shows young Britons stripped of their traditional reserve, with their sensitive light skins burnt from pink to red to dark red. G-strings are popular and bare breasts on the beaches are available for scrutiny.

The aesthetic codes are again very easily decoded, the imagery is sexually provocative and vocabulary is simplistic. The programme addresses audiences from the low-middle to working classes. This constitutes a significant segment of the population, and an extreme interest in the voyeurism and hedonism of *Ibiza Uncovered* documentaries attracts mass audiences.

POP CULTURE AS SUBVERSIVE?

'Aesthetics: a concept inherited from idealist philosophy, referring to principles of taste, especially good taste, and hence of beauty.'
John Hartley (1994: 6)

In order to discuss some developments in documentary aesthetics, it is necessary to look at the discourse of culture and to examine more closely the subject of 'high-brow' and 'low-brow' culture.

One of the reproaches of high-brow culture is its inherent elitism (see Hartley 1994). Removed from common experience it promotes and reinforces the notion of a chosen group of experts who are in a privileged position as interpreters of an artist's attention. The elite guardians assume the roles of refined and informed taste. This takes different forms such as critiques, debates, discussions, and is distributed in our culture through high-brow television programmes, designed to address audiences whose competences fall within the categories of high economic, social, cultural and symbolic capital. High-brow culture produces certain representations which ensure the status quo and the survival of the elite.

Pop culture, middle- and low-brow culture address audiences with lesser or different cultural capital. When pop culture subgroups break away and construct

figure 7
**Best of Ibiza Uncovered:
the party at manumission club**

their own aesthetics, these can be used as a means of social rebellion. This is what Walter Benjamin described as subversive non-violent resistance of social subjects, where they do not engage in revolution to overthrow dominant values/orders, but resist in oblique ways by constructing their own aesthetic concerns, as cultural sub-groups or alternative life styles, as in *Best of Ibiza Uncovered*. This programme might be read as a kind of hidden revolt of working-class girls and boys who go to Ibiza in search of jobs, fun holidays, freedom under the hot sun, sex, moonlight raves: a type of hedonistic lifestyle which is a 'no-go' zone back home. The groups depicted defy 'high-brow' cultural aesthetics by behaving in a spontaneous and provocative manner, and through this process of defiance their own new aesthetics are created.

figure 8
**hedonism as
subversive cultural
product?**

All documentaries are cultural artefacts and as such they are always representations of selected events, and not the events themselves. The level of credibility achieved by the *Big Brother* series depends on, among other things, individuals' awareness of the fact that the programmes are to an extent artificially constructed by the makers and are only representations of real events by *Big Brother*'s producers and editors (see Watson & Hill 1993).

Each spectator brings to his/her interpretation their own system of basic values, attitudes and beliefs. The more sceptical members of the audience are, the more likely they are to seek information in order to justify the contestants' positions as represented.

High/middle/low-brow aesthetics all coexist within the *Big Brother* programme. They are mediated through the producer's and editor's choice of content and style: the intent is to communicate with all kinds of people. Issues, such as past family relationships, careers, personal histories are represented in a seemingly spontaneous manner and within a domestic setting, which is traditionally a marker of middle/low-brow and feminine cultures. However, audiences with the necessary 'capital' can easily raise this entertainment to something verging on high-brow through interaction with the multimedia components of the production and through recognition of *Big Brother*'s pretence as authentic marker of events. Audiences' knowing comprehension of, and their participation in, this highly premeditated mixed genre of docu-soap, game-show, and new media experience in broadcasting (terrestrial and Web) can undermine traditional boundaries of high-, middle- and low-brow aesthetics. How and what sense the audience is going to make of the programme depends on how much of Bourdieu's economic, cultural, social and symbolic capital they possess.

We have seen, then, that a contemporary focus in documentary criticism centres around the spectator's position: the pleasure of watching and desire for watching, both of which are major rewards for audiences. Bourdieu's notions – about taste, jouissance, pure and naive gaze, economic/social/cultural and symbolic capital, cultural competences and life styles – are all implicated in, and meaningful to, the debate of high- versus low-brow culture. If the notion of jouissance implies a certain creative interaction between the documentary maker, the text and the spectator, it also paves a way towards an important democratisation of spectatorship and a speculation around 'preferred readings' (intent of producer) versus 'subversive readings' of audiences.

New debates around spectatorship include discussion about the advent of new technologies such as the Internet. Even though access to it is still restricted to certain groups of spectators, the possibility exists that access will be widened in the future.

This is what happened with previous technological achievements and applications. The Internet is a tool, and as such it is a means of production for many human activities, but it also allows for a wider and more interactive communication, as long as it belongs to everybody.

NOTES

1 *The Independent*, 'Friday Review', 15 September 2000, 1.

2 *Ibid*.

3 He often combined documentary and fiction in his work. See Price 1993: 277.

BIBLIOGRAPHY

Arato, A. (1982) Introduction to 'Esthetic Theory and Cultural Criticism', in *The Essential Frankfurt School Reader*. New York: Continuum, 183–224.

Benjamin, W. (1973) *Charles Baudelaire: A Lyric Poet in the Era of High Capitalism*. London: Verso.

Barthes, R (1977) *Image, Music, Text*. London: Fontana Press.

Bourdieu, P. (1980) 'The Aristocracy of Culture', in *Media, Culture and Society*. London: Academic Press, 225–54.

____ (1984) *Distinction: A Social Critique of the Judgement of Taste*. Cambridge: Harvard University Press.

Briggs, A. & P. Cobley (eds) (1998) *The Media: An Introduction*. London: Longman.Chambers, I. (1993) Popular Culture. London: Routledge.

Gration, G., J. Reilly & J. Titford (1988) *Introduction to Media Studies*. London: Macmillan.

Higson, A. (1995) *Waving The Flag: Constructing a National Cinema in Britain*. Oxford: Oxford University Press.

Horkheimer, M. & T. Adorno (1972) *Dialectic of Enlightenment*. New York: Seabury Press.

Maslow, A. (1970) *Motivation and Personality*. London: Harper & Row.

Morley, D. (1992) *Television, Audiences & Cultural Studies*. London: Routledge.

Nichols, B. (1985) 'The Voice of Documentary', *Film Quarterly*, 36, 3, 17–30

_____ (1992) *Ideology and the Image*. Bloomington: Indiana University Press.

Orwell, G. (1972) *Nineteen Eighty-Four*. London: Penguin.

O'Sullivan, T., J. Hartley, D. Saunders, M. Montgomery, & J. Fiske (1994) *Key Concepts in Communication and Cultural Studies*. London: Routledge.

Price, S. (1993) *Media Studies*. Harlow: Longman.

_____ (1996) *Communication Studies*. Harlow: Longman.

Seiter, E. (1999) *Television and New Media Audiences*. Oxford: Clarendon Press.

Silverstone, R. (1994) *Television and Everyday Life*. London: Routledge.

Varnedoe, K. & A. Gopnik (1990) *High and Low: Modern Art and Popular Culture*. Exhibition Catalogue. New York: Museum of Modern Art.

Watson, J. & A. Hill (1993) *Dictionary of Communication and Media Studies*. London: Edward Arnold.

Walker, J. (1999) *Who's Who in the Movies*. London: HarperCollins.

FURTHER READING

Allen, J. (1977) 'Self-Reflectivity in documentary', *Ciné Tracts*, 1, 2, 37–43.

Allen, R. C. (1999) 'Audience Orientated Criticism and Television', in *Channels of Discourse, Reassembled: Television and Contemporary Criticism*. North Carolina: University of North Carolina Press, 101–37.

De Lauretis, T. & S. Heath (eds) (1980) *The Cinematic Apparatus*. New York: St. Martin's Press.

Renov, M. (ed.) (1993) *Theorizing Documentary*. New York: Routledge.

Silverman, K. (1983) *The Subject of Semiotics*. London: Oxford University Press.

Tagg, J. (1988) *The Burden of Representation*. London: Macmillan.

USEFUL WEBSITES

- Documentary Box (journal devoted to covering recent trends in making and thinking about documentaries): www.city.yamagata.jp/yidff/docbox/docbox-html
- The Europe of cultural co-operation' (from 1989–2001): www.culture.coe.fr/Eurimages/bi/eurofilm/2001.html
- IDA International Documentary Association: www.documentary.org/
- Independent TV Services (ITVS) (established by US Congress to fund and promote programming that invokes creative risks and addresses the needs of underserved audiences, while granting artistic control to independent producers: www.namac.org/Directory/org-data/itvs.html
- *Big Brother*: www.bigbrother.terra.com/news/news/-main.html

   www.aber.ac.uk/media/BigBrother/press-release.html

   www.bigbrotheruk.xoasis.com/news.html
- BBC – UK TV Channel : www.bbc.co.uk

   www.bbc.co.uk/choice
- *Ibiza Uncovered*: www.tvlibrary.co.uk/pdb/p-16555.html
- David Attenborough: www-royalty.pp.asu.edu

   www.mbcnet.org/ETV/A/htmlA/attenborough/attenborough.htm
- Derek Jarman: www.unix.sbu.ac.uk/stafflog/derekjarman.html
- The New York International Documentary Festival: www.docfest.org/
- Television Audience Prediction: /www/braomstpr/cp/il/NCTT/portfolio/part04/pf4.20.1.htm

04 **production management** janice kearns

This chapter is a practical guide to production management and is largely based on my experience as a production manager in broadcast documentaries. Over the last ten years a lot of the details of making programmes in the industry have changed: technology has moved on, crews have become smaller, budgets have become smaller, but the fundamental principles of managing a production remain the same. It is these that can be, and should be, applied to college work as well.

Production management needs to be tackled with a positive attitude. Nothing is ever perfect and good production management is about making the best of the resources available. The best production managers are tenacious in pursuing their aims and explore every avenue to solve a problem.

Production management is principally about identifying, obtaining and managing all the practical resources to turn a film from an idea into an artefact. It is an area that novice film-makers are often tempted to skip over, regarding it as a dull and unnecessary encumbrance. It is dealt with in a shambolic manner as a sideline to the creative force of the production, and, because of this the initial vision is never fully realised. This is because the aims were not set out clearly and concretely at the start of the project and so they become muddied and lost along the way.

As creative people, film-makers sometimes mistakenly believe that inspiration alone will carry them through their production without the need for detailed planning. But planning is crucial if you are to realise the creative aims of your production. It is a skill that needs to be practised just as you would practice camera technique or editing. You may have developed a brilliant script and have a wealth of ideas about locations, camera angles and soundtracks, but if you do not plan your production, and plan it in detail, it will never be broadcast or screened.

Documentary production is always a collaboration requiring not only creative ideas, but technical and interpersonal skills, planning and management. It requires a lot of different resources in terms of people, equipment, time and places and these need to be carefully integrated. Juggling filming, scripting, location finding and all the other tasks you need to perform will not happen by some happy accident. Your initial creative idea will come to fruition only as a result of a lot of hard work and clever planning.

Let me stress at this stage that planning is not a linear process. Plans need to be constantly changed and adapted according to changing circumstances. This does not negate the planning process. The purpose of planning is to clearly identify our aim, work out the steps to take in order to achieve it and then decide the best way to perform those steps. Sometimes the best way is changed by changing circumstances and our plan should be able to adapt accordingly. If we do not make a plan we may not recognise how a change of circumstances affects our production and a vital element of the film may be lost.

In this chapter I have divided project management into three areas: Scheduling and Budgeting which deals with identifying resources; Pre-Production which looks at obtaining resources; and Managing Your Production which looks at the day to day running of the project.

SCHEDULING AND BUDGETING

Scheduling is creating a detailed plan of your project and budgeting is attaching costs to those plans. Scheduling and budgeting are the first steps in the practical planning of your production and involve identifying all the resources required to complete the project in terms of time, personnel, equipment, travel and subsistence. They are interdependent and so, before you create a budget, it is crucial that your project is developed to the treatment stage so that you can create a reasonably accurate schedule.

To start, divide your production into four distinct phases: Research and Development, Pre-Production, Production, and Post Production. In reality these phases may not be so distinct. Some of the production and post-production may run concurrently or you may be still involved in pre-production of some scenes while shooting is already underway. Your schedule can account for all this, but for clarity it is best to keep them separate at this stage.

Research and Development: most of your research and development will already be completed and so in terms of scheduling there will probably be little to do in this area. However it is worth reviewing the R & D phase and identifying the time you spent and the resources you used in terms of travel, books, telephone calls, meetings etc. All these will be legitimate budget expenses.

Pre-production: you need to schedule time for detailed planning and gathering resources (for example finding and contracting crew, hiring equipment, finding and securing locations, finding and gaining access to interviewees).

Production: this is the most complex phase to schedule. What looks like a very simple treatment can suddenly become very complex when it comes to planning the shoot (certain phases of the shoot may be co-dependent, certain scenes may need to be shot in a pre-defined order, there may be a number of locations etc). It is often helpful to group your scenes around the locations and assign a period of time for each scene, then look for any intrinsic order in the way the scenes are shot. This may require visiting a location more than once.

If you are documenting a specific event you may not have much control over your shooting schedule but will need to be guided by the event you are covering. Make sure you have a detailed outline of what is planned so that you can plan your shoot as accurately as possible. For example when working on *Astronauts* (Paul Berriff Productions/McDougall Craig for Channel 4, 1995), a documentary which followed the crew of a space shuttle through their training to the successful completion of their mission, it became clear that there were set events that we needed to film. In this case the shooting schedule was completely dependent on the training and launch schedule laid down by NASA. From the schedule they had created we had to choose the events we needed to cover in our film. Many of the events occurred several times in the schedule as the astronauts honed their skills, and so we had a degree of flexibility. But the mission itself – launch, time in space, and landing – was absolutely fixed (save for interventions from the weather, but more about contingencies later).

Such a predetermined schedule, rather than being restrictive, can actually be quite helpful. If you are the sole determiner of events or if you are covering something more spontaneous then planning your shoot can be tricky. If you cannot set precise timings for events set them within a broader time block, but be clear about how much of that block you will need to use. At this stage it is important to plan around the facts as they are currently, but be aware of factors which could cause a change in circumstances and look out for them.

Post-production: in terms of scheduling, post-production often seems elastic. It can always grow to fill the time available but it is also easy to forget to allow time for necessary processes such as logging rushes and copying tapes. Be aware of this. When scheduling post-production make sure you allow time for all the tasks and processes involved from reviewing and logging of rushes to the copying and reformatting of the final online*.

Once you have decided how long each section of a production will take you can begin to prepare a budget. Even at college level, this process is extremely important as it will help you identify your resourcing needs. You may find it useful to refer to the broadcast format budget used by independent producers (see appendix, below). It has different sections (called schedules) for specific budget areas and these serve as useful prompts to stop items being forgotten. While you are at college many of the facilities used in your production will be provided free of charge but it is worth getting into the habit of itemising and quantifying these (in terms of time) as you will find this experience useful when it comes to budgeting for your professional productions.

When budgeting professionally you should budget for everything you have included in the schedule and add a production fee of 10 to 15 per cent at the end. This is crucial. In professional productions this is your profit and is the money you will use to carry out the initial research on your next project. It may be expedient to make your first project at cost, just to get the thing made, and have one production under your belt. But once you are established, the production fee is a necessity to enable you to move from one production to the next. (I once worked on a production where an established production company agreed to waive the production fee and were nearly bankrupted because of it.)

Contingencies

If you are aware of any problems that may occur and could lengthen your schedule or cause additional costs plan for them now. In the industry you will find that sometimes funding bodies will accept these additional costs as budget contingencies. These are costs which do not form part of the main budget but which are agreed to be paid if the specific event identified occurs. For example in the *Astronauts* budget we built in some contingency money to deal with a delay in the launch.

When you have defined each element of the budget and schedule you need to actually assign dates to things. It can be useful to use a wall chart, or draw a time line on a large piece of paper and use differently coloured pieces of card to identify the individual elements.

It is at this stage that you can identify how the four phases of the production process fit together. They may simply form a linear path or you may find it necessary to begin logging and editing certain scenes before others have been shot. Make a detailed large-scale plan for your wall using colour coding to help identify individual elements and copy all the dates into your diary.

Funding

Whilst still at college you should investigate potential sources of sponsorship for your films. This is good practice for when you leave college, when you will find that the most difficult part of the production is getting funding. First-time film-makers should fully exploit the range of initiatives set up regionally for new directors, new writers etc. Broadcasters often fund these directly and it is worth telephoning your local ITV company to find out what schemes, if any, they run. The BBC and Channel 4 also have short slots reserved for novice film-makers and many broadcasters run competitions to discover new talent.

The thing about funding is to contact as many people as possible: regional arts councils, the film council, anyone you can think of. Be prepared with a pitch in case you get the opportunity to talk about your project over the phone and make sure you have your budget handy. Most of the time any funding you get will be small but sometimes it is possible to get funding from more than one source to bump up the budget a bit (called 'pack of cards' financing). You must be clear to any financier (and in your own mind) the proportion of the budget they are funding and what that entitles them to in terms of rights, screenings or broadcasts.

PRE-PRODUCTION

During the research phase of your project you may have already identified the main protagonists of your film. If not you will certainly have identified the 'types' you are looking for (for example people who will articulate a specific point of view or perform a specific role). In the pre-production phase you need to pin down the individual characters in your film. This is the case even if you are filming an organisation.

During pre-production on *The Nick* (Paul Berriff Productions for Channel 4, 1994), a series about East Leeds police station, we identified 'characters' that we would follow during filming. These were people who were articulate in front of the camera and open to being filmed. People who are not self-conscious in front of the camera are crucial to the success of projects like this. And it is important that you try to put people at ease. Make sure they understand fully what the programme is about and what is required of them. If they trust you they are much more likely to be relaxed in front of a camera. The main focus of *The Nick* was community policing and so we picked a couple of beat officers from each shift to concentrate the majority of our filming on. This, we hoped, would provide continuity to the stories we filmed. During the course of our shoot some of our focus shifted. Drug abuse became an increasingly important story and so we adapted our original plan so that we could cover some officers in the undercover drug squad.

Location finding

When you are looking for a specific location it is always worth making known to as many people as possible the kind of place you are looking for. Tourist Information offices can also be very helpful, but generally your best bet is to use your eyes.

When you have found a possible location you will need to do a detailed recce. If possible take the key personnel with you when you do this. They will be able to view the location from their specialism and if they are already familiar with the location it could save valuable time on your shoot.

Here are the things to look out for:

Light: What is the available light? If you are relying on daylight – what time of day do you need to be there for the optimum conditions? If the light is artificial – what is the colour temperature* of the light? What additional lighting will the location need? What camera filters or gels will you require? Are there sufficient power points? Can the location be lit safely? When considering light and light sources you need to be very clear about the style of your shots. If you are looking at a realistic approach then it may be important to have plenty of available light, however if your shots are more stylised and require lots of set-up lighting effects then available light may not be important but plenty of power points will.

Sound: When you enter your location stop and listen. Make a note of all the extraneous sounds. Common problems include: traffic, aircraft, air conditioning, lifts, PA systems, telephones, electrical appliances. Try to work out a way round the problem (for example, can the air conditioning be turned off for short periods during shooting, can you film at a time when traffic levels are lower, can the phones be disconnected during filming?). You need to work through these issues at the scouting stage so you know if the location is viable.

Access: Work out the best way of getting your equipment and crew into the location. Is there parking nearby? Is there a lift you can use? Will there be a trolley or sack barrow available or will you need to bring one of your own?

Permission: Lastly and most importantly, make sure you have the express permission of the person who owns or controls the site. You can use a formal location agreement, but generally a simple letter outlining what you will be doing, when and for how long, signed by the relevant person is best. This is the letter you can then show to the officious doorman who tries to bar your way. Make sure too, that you have a telephone number for the person granting permission, that you can reach them on at the time of your shoot. Then if there are any problems you can contact them directly and hopefully everything will be sorted out quickly.

Finding and hiring crew

At college contracting a crew is not a problem! Once you are working in the industry, more formal procedures come into play. In the industry, where you find your crew really depends on the kind of production you are making and the kind of budget you have. There are several published guides which should help you find personnel in your area. BECTU, for example, publishes regional directories of crew. These usually give a brief outline of an individual's experience and can be an invaluable starting point. Film commissions will also have lists of freelances working in the locality.

Ring local production companies or facilities houses for recommendations. For very low-budget productions it may be worth advertising for crew on www.shootingpeople.org which is a web-based noticeboard mostly aimed at getting crew seeking experience together with low-budget film-makers. You may also find the website useful for finding work experience while you are at college.

Whether you are hiring professionals or relying on favours from friends always make sure the person you are hiring can do the job you are asking of them. Always get a CV and talk to them about their previous experience. Make sure their experience is relevant and ask to see samples of their work. Remember, just because a camera operator can shoot beautifully lit drama set-ups does not necessarily mean that she/he can shoot fast-moving fly-on-the-wall footage – and this is not something you can wait until your shoot to find out.

You also need to make sure that your crew members are fully au fait with the equipment you will be using. It is essential to choose the equipment in consultation with the crew, or they may be able to supply equipment themselves. Often camera operators and sound recordists have their own equipment and you can hire them and their equipment as a single package. Go through your storyboards or treatment with the crew and agree the equipment you will need in each scene. A big bulky kit may not be practical if you are capturing footage on the hoof but in a formal interview setting a large camera may give you a more professional appearance. You also need to bear in mind the way the material will be post-produced. (For example, if sound and picture are generated separately do you have a reliable system for post syncing the material?)

MANAGING YOUR PRODUCTION

The day-to-day managing of your production requires good organisational skills and a pragmatic approach to problems. Be assured of one thing: however carefully you have planned things there will always be something and some stage that will upset the apple cart.

For example, after all my careful planning on the *Astronauts* project there was a furlough in the middle of a shooting phase and the whole of NASA shut down for a week because their funds had been frozen. This meant we had a UK crew on location, with no astronaut training to film and no way of knowing how long the situation would continue. Of course we adapted our schedule to film some social events with the astronauts and do some pick-up shots. But it was a tough judgement call to decide whether we should cut our losses and go home or to wait it out. This situation was something we could never have foreseen and this is often the way with film production – expect the unexpected. The important thing is to be clear about what you need to achieve and know where you are in terms of achieving it. An invaluable tool in doing this is a diary.

When you finalise your planned schedule write all your plans into your diary. So that during each day of your production you know what needs to be done. Then as you complete each task tick it off in the diary. If there are any tasks that you do not complete, reschedule them for the following day. If you delegate tasks to others write a note in your diary to check on the progress of the task. This is all very simple and straightforward but an absolutely invaluable way of keeping track of your production.

Communication

As the production manager, your most important job is as a communicator: keeping everyone up to speed with what is happening and what will be happening next. The most important thing is to know how to contact people so always make sure that you have your book of contacts with you. This should include contact details for all the crew (phone, address, mobile, e-mail – as many different points of contact as you can).

Make sure you have contact details for local facilities houses, stock and equipment suppliers. You will also need to know numbers for local taxis, restaurants, takeaways and hotels. Also make sure that you have all the details of the schedule for the day, and the following day if there is one. These are called 'Call Sheets' and should be distributed among the crew so that everyone knows what they are doing.

The call sheet should contain details of the day's shooting, with times, locations and crew members required on location. It should outline the scenes, interviews and so on to be filmed in each location. Most importantly for your crew it should outline where and when meal breaks will take place. People work a lot better if they know that their needs are being looked after. As production manager you need to make sure that your crew is fed, watered, informed and happy.

It is vital when managing your production that you take your responsibilities, in terms of the health, safety and ethical treatment of those you encounter, seriously. Most of this is common sense and involves keeping people informed of your intentions and not taking risks with people's safety in order to get shots.

You should ask all your contributors to sign a release form – this should state that they understand the nature of your production and assert no right under copyright law in the contribution they make.

If you are filming in a public place and there is any possibility that you may cause an obstruction, inform the local police of what you are doing. In most cases you will find them very helpful. It is always worth taking out public liability insurance as well as insurance for crew and equipment. Colleges and industry commissioning bodies will usually take care of this for you. Be aware that many facilities houses will not hire you equipment unless you can demonstrate that you have insurance to cover it.

It is essential that any agreements that you make with crew, contributors or suppliers are put down in writing. For college productions a letter written in clear language, stating what has been agreed, should be sufficient. Professionally, production managers use agreements such as those drawn up by the Producers Alliance for Cinema and Television (PACT). They produce specimen documents for contracting crew, contributor's release, location agreements etc, and have a sliding scale of fees depending on the size of your production.

On location

When the crew is very small, it is often necessary for the production manager to act as a production assistant and fixer on location. This means that you will be responsible for shot listing, collecting release forms, organising, transport, meal breaks and so forth, and generally making sure that everything runs smoothly. In industry I have invariably worked as part of a four-person crew: Director/camera, camera assistant, sound recordist and me. At college, a small crew will also be the case. In this scenario everyone needs to work well together as a team. It is important that the crew's physical needs are taken care of, for them to give their best. It is part of making people feel they are valued and their skills respected.

Contingencies: the pragmatic approach to disasters

One thing that can be guaranteed is that not everything in your production will go as planned. It is important to realise this from the outset. At some stage you will be faced with the prospect of making the best of what may appear at the time to be a major disaster. When this happens there are a number of things you should do:

1. Keep a cool head and try not to get emotional about the situation.

2. Accept that it has happened – do not waste time wishing things were different.

3. Look for the best solution. Some people ignore the best solution because they are looking for the perfect solution. You need to be pragmatic. Keep in mind what you need to achieve and work out the best way to achieve it. It may require you to move location, find another interviewee or slightly refocus your project.

4. Do not dismiss alternatives as impossible until you have explored them fully. Alternatives may be difficult, require a lot of additional time and effort, but this does not necessarily make them impossible. When exploring alternatives you need to keep positive and develop a 'can do' attitude rather than cast yourself in the role of victim and give up.

During the filming of *Animal Squad Undercover* (Paul Berriff Productions for Channel 4, 1992) a very frightening incident happened to our crew. We had been filming the RSPCA undercover team following a consignment of live sheep from Dover to their eventual destination in Italy. We had planned a grand finale to the programme as the RSPCA men confronted the lorry driver and abattoir staff at the end of a three-day journey. But as the film crew arrived at the abattoir they were violently attacked by workers. The film was confiscated and the crew made a hasty retreat. Everyone was very shaken by events and although what happened would make a good story, we now had no footage of the end of our journey.

Director/cameraman Paul Berriff was already formulating a plan. We would re-film the part of the journey where the lorry turned off the main road and go to the top of a large hill at the edge of the town to film a panorama of the area. This could then be intercut with some reconstructions of the crew running back to their cars. Voice-over could be used to explain what had happened.

It was a good solution. The secret of finding good solutions to difficult situations is largely one of acceptance. It is important to accept the situation as is. Not to keep wishing things were different. Once you have accepted and understood the situation as it is, you need to pragmatically look for the best solution. Do not look for the perfect solution because you will never find it. Look for the best way out of a bad situation. If something cannot be done then it cannot be done, but make sure you have exhausted every avenue before you throw in the towel.

When making *Astronauts* we managed to get NASA to agree to having one of our 16mm film cameras on board the space shuttle for the astronauts to shoot on-board footage. NASA was very nervous about letting this footage go off site without its personnel viewing it first, and was proposing to develop it 'in house'. We were very nervous about NASA doing this as super 16 was not a format it was used to using and if the film was damaged in the processing stage it would be useless to us. We tried everything to persuade NASA to have the exposed film sent to our labs in Leeds (at the time one of the few specialist super 16 labs in the world). NASA would not be budged.

In the end the only way we could persuade NASA to release the footage was if I personally couriered the film stock to Leeds, waited while it was processed and printed and then brought it all the way back so that NASA could view it. It seems like an extraordinary length to go to, a trip from Florida to Leeds and back to Houston, but it was crucial that we did not lose the footage and so that is what I did.

Sometimes you will need to do things which, to a sane individual, will seem ridiculously convoluted or time-intensive to save your film, but often it is going that extra mile that makes the film.

Copyright

If all the material in your film has been generated by yourself then you should not have any problems with copyright. You (or your college) will hold copyright in the film.

Things become more complicated if you include material generated by other people. If, for example, you wish to include pre-recorded music or archive footage in your film you will need to obtain copyright clearance. This can be a protracted process. The best place to start when trying to gain permission is the source of the material. The broadcaster, record company or footage library should be able to enlighten you as to the ownership of the material and may be able to clear the material for you. For copyright clearance of music contact the Mechanical Copyright Protection Society (MCPS) who will be able to advise you.

The Institute of Amateur Cinematographers (IAC) also runs a scheme for its members which may be useful while you are at college but be aware that this only covers amateur exhibition of your work. If you are planning to exploit your work in professional settings then clearing the copyright for the pre-recorded music plastered all over your soundtrack can be a real headache and very expensive.

At the end of the production...

Immediately after completing your production, sort through all your paperwork one last time. If you have made the production for broadcast, the broadcaster will require that you fill in a 'programme as completed' form which records all important information about the production: title, length, a summary of content, end credits, contributors, copyright material used. Even if you do not have to complete a form like this, it is as well to record all these facts for your own information. If you do have to fill one in make sure you keep a copy for yourself. Then, if there is any need to contact a contributor in the future or you need to check any detail of your film, it is all there in black and white. Keep this information with your master tapes, release forms, location agreements, contact names and addresses of crew, cast etc in a box file for future reference. You never know when you might need them.

Make sure you write a personal thank you to anyone who has helped you during the production – your crew as well as interviewees, people who helped with your research and anyone who provided a service for you during the course of the production. People like to have their work recognised and they will feel more kindly disposed towards helping you in future productions if you let them know how much you appreciated their efforts. They may also be in a position to recommend you for other work or offer you work themselves. If you treat contributors well, your production can be a useful source of future contacts.

I hope this chapter will prove useful as you set about managing your productions. If you are to take one guiding principle away from this chapter it should be communication. Communicate fully and honestly with your crew, your contributors, your suppliers and funders. Treat people in a decent and ethical way and be assertive about your requirements. People will respond more favourably to you if you are clear about what is needed and are confident enough to communicate that effectively.

APPENDIX

SCHEDULE 1 – summary of broadcast budget used by independent producers

Programme title:
Programme number:

Synopsis:

Number of programmes   Length of programmes   mins

Production Co.:

Address:

Telephone: Fax: Email:

Key personnel:

	Date	Date	No. of weeks	
Development:	to			weeks
Pre-production:	to			weeks
Production:	to			weeks
Post-production	to			weeks
Delivery Dates:				
		Total number of weeks		weeks

Studios:
Locations:
Labs/Facility Houses:

Programmes originated on:
Programmes delivered on:
Stereo/Mono* sound:
Has an M&E been budgeted for?:
Other Details:

SCHEDULE 2 – industrial relations

Please list those unions on which the figures are based:
(Writers/Equity/MU/BECTU/PACT)

Number of UK transmissions fully cleared within the budget:
Other rights cleared (please detail)

SCHEDULE 3 – cost summary

Direct costs and overheads:
Production Fee @   %:
Contingencies:
(detail specific & general)
Completion Guarantee (if appropriate)
Guarantor:

TOTAL COST:

FINANCE SUMMARY
Proposed Funding: Broadcaster:
                            Other:
                                              Total Funding:

SCHEDULE 4 – budget summary

Ref:	Direct Costs and overheads:	
5	Story/Script	£
6	Producer/Director	
7	Artists	
8	Presenters/Interviewees	
9	Production Unit Salaries	
10	Assistant Directors/Continuity	
11	Crew – Camera	

12	Crew – Sound
13	Crew – Lighting
14	Crew – Art Department
15	Crew – Wardrobe/Make up/Hair
16	Crew – Editing
17	Crew – Second Unit
18	Salary and Wage Related Overheads
19	Materials – Art Department
20	Materials – Wardrobe/Makeup/Hair
21	Production Equipment
22	Facility Package Arrangements
23	Studios/Outside broadcast
24	Other production facilities
25	Film/Tape Stock
26	Picture/Sound Post Production – Film
27	Picture/Sound Post Production – Tape
28	Archive Material
29	Rostrum/Graphics
30	Music (copyright/performance)
31	Travel/Transport
32	Hotel/Living
33	Other Production Costs
34	Insurance/Finance/Legal
35	Production Overheads
36	Theatrical Performances
37	Continuation sheets
	TOTAL DIRECT COSTS AND OVERHEADS

FURTHER READING

Gates, R. (1999) *Production Management for Film and Video*. Oxford: Focal Press.

Jones, C. & G. Jolliffe (1996) *The Guerilla Film Makers Handbook*. London: Cassell.

Honhanther, E. L. (2001) *Complete Film Production Handbook*. Oxford: Focal Press.

USEFUL WEBSITES

Online directories

www. theknowledgeonline.com – the Knowledge Online Directory

www.kays.co.uk – website for Kays production manual

www.kemps411.com – website for Kemps International Directory

www.4rfv.co.uk – regional film and video directory

Professional organisations

www.pact.co.uk – Producers Alliance for Cinema and Television

www.bectu.co.uk – Broadcasting, Entertainment, Cinematograph and Theatre Union

www.dga.org – Directors Guild of America

Miscellaneous

www.bfi.org.uk – British Film Industry

www.afi.com – American Film Industry

www.britfilmcom.co.uk – British Film Commission

www.rts.org.uk – Royal Television Society

www.filmcouncil.org.uk – Film Council

www.fvi.org.uk – Film & Video Institute

www.cinematographer.com – American Society of Cinematographers

www.fvi.org.uk/iacframeset.html – Institute of Amateur Cinematographers www.mcps.co.uk – Mechanical Copyright Protection Society

www.aivf.org – Association of Independent Video and Filmmakers

www.ifp.org – Independent Feature Project

www.shortfilmbureau.com – for advice on funding and production

www.shootingpeople.com – web-based newsgroup for film and video production

www.cinematography.net – web-based discussion group

www.broadcastnow.co.uk – industry news and information

www.reelscreen.com – information on film and television

www.industrycentral.net – resources for the motion picture and television professional

05 **documentary cinematography** william garrison

As a producer, I am always intrigued by the response of audiences to my work and the work of others. This response is often surprising. Things I consider clever, creative, or beautiful, are often ill-perceived by others. Conversely, programmes I consider banal attract huge audiences and huge profits. Audiences can be fickle with individuals expressing different values, likes and dislikes. Among all this diversity of opinion I have observed that there is one universal value that all viewers share – a perception of quality. Virtually all viewers, from children to mature adults, can perceive quality. They may disagree about the content, meaning, and aesthetics, but viewers most often agree about quality of the visual expression.

This perception of quality reflects rudimentary elements of craftsmanship. Everyone perceives the difference between a motion picture film and a televised serial drama. Everyone perceives the difference between a news segment and a documentary. Each of these examples exemplifies different production values that create a sense of perceived quality. Both the serialised drama and the motion picture film are scripted dramas, often produced by talented writers, actors and directors. They differ in the attention to detail and quality of craftsmanship. Similarly, the documentary and the news segment share many elements but differ greatly in the quality of experience.

Although these examples differ on many levels, the choice of production techniques and quality of craftsmanship are among the most revealing.

Documentary film-makers often perceive that the very nature of the medium in which they work precludes quality. This chapter will attempt to dispel the notion that because documentary film-making is rooted in reality and truth, it must forgo the production techniques and values viewers often associate with high-quality programmes. Film-makers have at their disposal an array of tools and techniques to create and manipulate moving images. All film-makers, whether documentary or dramatic, need to understand these techniques in order to apply them, or choose not to apply them.

Whatever style, techniques, or methodologies a film-maker chooses to apply, it is important that they are applied effectively to support the objectives. This is the difference between quality and mediocrity. This is the difference between effective images that advance the film-maker's efforts, or ineffective images that detract. Viewers expect quality and craftsmanship and often have little patience for mediocrity. Whatever the nature of your film, whatever your intent, audiences will be more receptive to its content if it is well crafted. This chapter hopes to illuminate some of the camera techniques that, when applied appropriately, will increase the ability of the film-maker to affect his/her audience.

Film-making is essentially a visual art form and its effectiveness rests, to a large degree, on the quality of the images. This is true across the spectrum of film-making from fly-on-the-wall documentary to big-budget Hollywood films. To illustrate this point I have chosen four films; two documentaries and two dramas. *Titicut Follies* (Bridgewater Film Co., 1967) and *The Thin Blue Line* (C4/American Playhouse/Program Development Co., 1988) are seminal films in documentary history representing polar extremes in documentary film-making. *Titicut Follies* is a fly-on-the-wall, observational work, while the director of *The Thin Blue Line* uses actors and dramatic techniques to illuminate truths. The two fiction films I have chosen are also polar extremes in narrative film. *Gladiator* (Universal/Dreamworks, 2000) is an exquisitely crafted film that excels because of the naturalness of its images and the use of documentary techniques to create tension and excitement. *This is Spinal Tap* (Mainline/Embassy, 1984) is a highly contrived comedy in the guise of documentary film. It lampoons documentary film-making by applying and exploiting the conventions and clichés of documentary film-making to great comic effect. These four examples illustrate how the film-maker can evoke powerful responses in the audience through effective choice of techniques and how this choice is informed by a broad understanding of cinematic technique without regard to genre.

PASSIVE VERSUS ACTIVE CINEMATOGRAPHY

Cinematographers in all genres are concerned with the same things; composition, lighting, camera placement, focal length of the lens, exposure, and camera movement. All these issues apply to both documentary and fiction film-making. The difference among genres lies not in the production techniques, but rather the degree to which the director has control over these and other elements.

The director of a big-budget fiction film, such as Ridley Scott in *Gladiator*, has the wherewithal to control every detail from elaborate computer-generated sets to precise camera placement and lighting. The documentary director has much less control, although these same elements must weigh heavily in every decision made. In *Titicut Follies*, Frederick Wiseman makes powerful choices in camera placement, focal length, use of available light, and composition while also minimising his influence on the action. *Gladiator* and *Titicut Follies* are both powerful films because of the skill of the film-makers in creating effective images using the cinematic tools at their disposal. Regardless of the degree of influence a director has over the subject, the same cinematic principles and techniques apply. Obviously, *Gladiator* and *Titicut Follies* were not shot in the same way. *Gladiator* made extensive use of sets, both real and virtual, and Wiseman would have been unable to use large lighting instruments, lay dolly track, or rehearse shots. There are a great many differences in practical terms between documentary and dramatic film-making, but in principle, the language of the moving image is the same. The production techniques that support this language can be applied across genres.

The choices to apply or not apply a technique must be made actively. For instance, a cinematographer may choose to shoot hand-held because it creates an effect of immediacy and tension appropriate for the scene. Scott made this choice for many of the battle scenes in *Gladiator.* Errol Morris chose to apply techniques usually associated with film noir in *The Thin Blue Line*. Rob Reiner uses documentary and dramatic techniques in *This is Spinal Tap* to create a documentary illusion, and Wiseman's careful use of natural light, camera placement, lenses, and composition in *Titicut Follies* resulted in images that can be associated with fiction films as well. *Gladiator* is a striking film in its naturalness. Light seems to flow gently across interior scenes. It is a natural light, coloured and contoured to support the director's intent and is always motivated – well motivated – by implication coming from a window, door, or candle. In *Titicut Follies*, Wiseman's shots have strong, powerful lighting with hard shadows cast across the features of people's faces. He achieves this without a single light – simply through careful camera placement to best utilise light coming through windows.

These directors made active choices to apply or not apply production techniques from the full cinematic spectrum. Too often, film-makers make passive choices. The camera operator chooses to shoot hand-held because the tripod is too heavy. Action is filmed with bland overhead light because of inadequate planning or unimaginative camera placement. These are passive choices and invariably poor choices. Every decision regarding production techniques should be made actively and must be informed by a broad understanding of those techniques. Every choice to apply, or not apply a technique, will affect the way audiences respond to the images and their content.

CAMERA

Planning the scene

The script for a fiction film is typically divided into scenes and each scene broken down into shots. This breakdown gives the director the opportunity to exert complete control over all elements that make up each shot. Set design, camera placement, special effects, and the performances of the actors can be planned with precision using storyboards and other devices. What appears on screen is often the result of careful planning.

Students of documentary production often approach their subjects with the opposite view of production. They assume that the documentary director has little control and simply responds to the scene that unfolds before the camera. This attitude invariably results in mediocrity for many reasons. Shots are ill-conceived, scenes do not edit well, lighting is poor, sound is poor, and the audiences perceive the work as mediocre. Mediocrity becomes a barrier between the audience and the content, and the director's vision, intent, and window on a truth become obscured. Planning is essential in order to avoid mediocrity. Planning can occur on many levels and to many degrees. Not all situations can be anticipated and planned; however, the more forethought and planning one puts into a project, the more likely the outcome will be engaging and compelling. Even naturalistic, observational documentaries benefit from planning.

Wiseman gives the impression that his films simply record events happening before the camera. But which events did Wiseman choose and why did he choose them? What did he know about the locations? How did he expect the participants to behave? All film-makers must make decisions about when and where to film and which production techniques to apply. These choices are always better made with some forethought and planning.

Anticipating action

Pre-production techniques used in fiction films apply equally well to documentary, although they may be applied to differing degrees. The fiction-film director will have a list of shots, or shot sheet for each location. In documentary, this shot list is equally useful, although rather than resulting from months of planning, it is created in short order and often on the fly. Using your knowledge of why you have chosen a location and the anticipated action, you can develop a shot list. This list is very important and provides a baseline and checklist to work against. At the end of a shoot, you can review the shotlist to ensure you have the images you need and the coverage for editing.

The documentary film-maker who goes to a location to 'get some footage' is inviting mediocrity. The film-maker has made choices about what to film and why. These choices need to be clear because they will guide the many creative, aesthetic, and technical decisions that must be made. The film-maker probably has some idea of what will happen and how it will fit into the narrative or aesthetic structure they are creating. This structure may change during the course of the project, but it must begin at some point. This understanding is the basis of a plan that will foster sound decisions regarding camera technique.

Documentary production can be very unpredictable. Unlike the fiction-film director, the documentary film-maker must constantly evaluate the scene and make changes to the plan. Action seldom unfolds as imagined and the camera operator and director need to be prepared to adapt and move quickly as action unfolds. The difference between documentary and fiction production lies not in the plan but rather the speed at which the plan is revised. The director is constantly thinking in terms of shots and scenes. When the action changes, the shotlist is adapted immediately. This may not happen on paper, but it must happen none-the-less.

Choosing camera placements

Once a location is chosen and action anticipated, the director begins to think about how this action will be interpreted on film. Camera placement is one of the key decisions and needs to take into account action, layout of the location, available light, and the ability of the crew to move during the action. This is seldom a simple decision and requires much thought. Poor placement can result in poor compositions, missed action, and can even disrupt the course of events.

Typically, the director has a scene in mind that will be created in editing from shots acquired at this location. This usually involves several set-ups, or camera placements, to cover the action and to allow the creative composition necessary for the scene. Camera placement is important because it will determine the initial position of the tripod and any additional lighting used. By planning each setup, lights can be adjusted for each angle so that when the subjects enter the location, everything is ready. Under most production situations, this is just the starting point and the director must adapt as the action unfolds. If the lighting and camera placements were carefully planned, the director will have sufficient flexibility to adapt to changing action easily.

Choosing the camera position is exceedingly important. It affects shot composition, lighting, focal length, and a host of other factors that affect how the shot looks. Poorly thought out placement invites mediocrity. There are two good examples of camera placement in *Spinal Tap*. Most of the camera work in this film is intentionally bad and laden with clichés for comic effect. Occasionally, however, Rob Reiner shows his brilliance as a director of documentaries.

Ian Faith, band manager, learns that the Spinal Tap album has not been released because the cover is deemed too offensive for the US market. He learns this in a conversation with Bobbie Flekman, a record company executive, in a scene that begins with a two-shot. The scene is lit from an overhead light almost directly behind the camera and the shot is wide. The effect is bland and benign. As the conflict intensifies, the camera moves to a close-up of Ian and a close-up of Bobbie. These shots are 'over-the-shoulder' and very close to the axis of the conversation. Also, the lighting that was initially flat is now hard and full of contrast because the light is now at 90° to the camera view. As the conflict dissipates, the camera moves back to the original two-shot with soft, flat lighting. This powerful change of mood was achieved through the placement of the camera through three setups and the use of different focal length lenses.

Scene direction

In all but the most naturalistic format, the director has some opportunity to direct the scene and influence performances. Most documentary directors would agree that once a subject becomes accustomed to the camera and crew they can easily adapt to small suggestions from the director. These small changes can greatly improve the quality of images by allowing the director to take advantage of a location.

These suggestions might take the form of, 'Would you mind sitting at this table instead?' or, 'I would prefer if you could stand on that side of the window.' These sorts of careful suggestions allow the director to vastly improve the images through careful use of the location while minimising their interaction with the subject. The degree to which one interacts with the subject is always contingent on the rhetorical style chosen. If your style allows some direction, a small amount can have tremendous impact.

Choosing the camera

Much has been written about the value of miniature digital cameras. Their small size, low-light capabilities, low cost and resemblance to consumer cameras have created new opportunities for the documentary film-maker. But the advantage of these cameras is not as great as one thinks. They are ideal in difficult situations where the director chooses to use a minimum amount of equipment to minimise interaction with the subject. Fly-on-the-wall, or covert recording can benefit from these cameras.

However, the size advantage offered by mini-digital cameras is often overstated. The camera is only one component in the professional production kit, and it is by no means the largest. Lighting instruments, rifle microphones with wind-screens, boom poles, and tripods, can be much more cumbersome than the camera. Reducing the camera size by 50 per cent does not make a significant impact on the amount of equipment required.

The complexity of a shoot is often the result of the quantity of equipment required, and not the size. Effective lighting may require five instruments, umbrellas, reflectors, C-stands, silks, etc. Sound recording may require three wireless microphones, one rifle mic on a boom, and a mixer. A sturdy tripod may be necessary for long shots. By this point, the size of the camera makes little difference.

Mini-digital cameras generally have inferior picture quality, they can be difficult to operate, and often lack professional features essential for high-quality production. They have limited tonal ranges and poor chroma detail. Programmes that are shot with mini-digital cameras tend to have a rough, unpleasant aesthetic quality due to their limitations and the way they are used. Unless this aesthetic is justified, directors are well advised to use professional equipment whenever possible.

The professional camera

The professional camera has two principal qualities that distinguish it from 'prosumer' mini-digital cameras. Firstly, they tend to produce higher quality images by design. The lenses are usually better, and image sensors and electronics tend to be optimised for quality with fewer design compromises to reduce manufacturing costs. The digital encoding and recording formats are generally superior. Professional cameras using Betacam, DVC-Pro 50, Digital-S, Digi-Betacam, or Beta-SX produce better recorded images than Mini-DV, DVCAM or DVC-Pro.

The second important advantage of professional cameras is ease of use. 'Prosumer' cameras are much simpler to operate on an amateur level. Auto-focus, auto-iris, and vibration dampening can help the unskilled camera operator to achieve reasonable results. But for the professional operator, 'prosumer' cameras are difficult to use in creative ways to achieve high-quality results. Let us take a look at a few central concerns:

The Lens: The professional camera has a well-marked lens indicating focus, zoom, and iris. Having direct control over these features is very important. For instance, the focus ring on a professional lens is mechanically connected to the lens elements. With experience, an operator can track focus of a moving subject purely by feel. Prosumer cameras use electronic focus mechanisms that provide little feedback to the operator.

Audio Recording: Professional camcorders provide multiple audio inputs for balanced line and microphone sources. Each channel is individually controlled with professional level indicators.

Exposure: Poor exposure is one of the first indications of mediocre camera work. Obtaining properly exposed shots is difficult and requires considerable skill and experience. The iris and shutter controls, and the viewfinder of professional cameras provide the operator far greater control over exposure.

Colour Balance: Professional cameras typically have two colour balance memories per filter. With these tools, the director and operator can survey a scene, record colour balances in various areas where filming is likely to occur, and then quickly switch from setting to setting as the action unfolds. Colour balance is an important aesthetic tool and is essential to achieving effective and engaging images.

Accessories: Professional cameras are designed to accommodate professional accessories such as matte boxes, interchangeable lenses, wireless receivers, french flags, etc.

Mini-digital cameras

Mini-DV cameras can produce satisfactory images when used with care and attention to detail. Many of the limitations can be overcome by using the manual control features to ensure that exposure, focus, audio and colour balance are set correctly for each shot. These cameras tend to be very sensitive to overexposure, producing broad white patches. Achieving quality results is possible, but requires experience, practice, patience, careful lighting, and attention to detail.

Exposure

Achieving correct exposure is never easy. This is as true for high-budget films as well as low-budget documentaries. The professional cinematographer is concerned with capturing tonal values that best support the aesthetic and dramatic intent of the director for each scene. The documentary camera operator faces exactly the same task, but with much less control over light sources and action. Exposure is about utilising the dynamic range of the camera, from black to white, to create effective and evocative images.

Auto-iris: All video cameras come equipped with auto-iris. This automatic exposure setting is optimised to produce satisfactory images most of the time. Auto-iris is set electronically by the camera according to priorities set by the manufacturer. The iris is typically set to ensure that there are areas of white and areas of black within the scene with shades of grey and colour falling somewhere between. In many situations, auto-iris produces acceptable results. But what if the scene is primarily white? Auto-iris will produce an underexposed grey image. What if the scene is primarily black, such as a stage play? Auto-iris will produce an over exposed image. What if subjects within the frame move or the camera pans? Auto-iris adjusts creating exposure shifts within the shot. The auto-iris function does not make aesthetic judgements. It does not compensate for bright sources and dark areas. It does not produce creative results and seldom supports the aesthetic intent of the director. Auto-iris should never be used except in extreme situations.

Setting exposure: Setting the correct exposure requires practice and experience. There is no simple guide because good exposure results from a full understanding of the limitations of the camera, the dynamics of the scene, and the aesthetic intent of the director.

Limitations of the camera: The human eye adapts and interprets a far greater dynamic range than the camera. Consequently, the camera operator must interpret the scene and make decisions about what is important and how it is to be portrayed within the limited dynamic range of the camera. Imagine two subjects having a conversation by a kitchen window. The eye reveals detail in the faces, detail in the shadows around the sink, and detail in the scene outside the window. The camera, however, is capable of revealing only one of these three areas. If exposure is set correctly for the exterior scene viewed through the window, faces fall nearly black and the shadow detail around the sink is invisible. If exposure is set for the faces, the outside scene is grossly overexposed and the shadow areas are still black. If exposure is set for the shadows, the exterior scene is completely lost and faces are overexposed. Setting exposure in this instance requires choice and compromise between the limitations of the camera and the intent of the director.

Scene dynamics: The feature-film cinematographer applies careful lighting to ensure that all areas of the scene have the required illumination to achieve the intended effect. Exposure is set to ensure that the chosen tonal values are correctly captured on film. In documentary production, the director often has little control over lighting and action. Consequently, subjects move in and out of different lighting conditions creating immense challenges for the camera operator.

The operator can anticipate these changes and adjust the iris manually as action unfolds, or the operator can choose a compromise setting that attempts to cover both dark and light areas. This can be difficult to achieve as dark areas will appear underexposed and bright areas overexposed. Careful exposure in these dynamic situations is essential.

Aesthetic intent: Exposure also depends on the aesthetic intent of the director. Video images are typically exposed to include both areas of black and white utilising the full dynamic range of the medium. This may not be appropriate. The director may wish to create a sense of ambiguity or fear by leaving large areas of the image in darkness. The director may wish to accentuate different elements by using exposure creatively, such as silhouette, or may wish to expose for bright areas in a high-contrast situation to reveal shapes and contours that would be lost through normal exposure. Exposure affects the way textures appear. It affects colours and saturation. It affects how viewers perceive the subjects.

Exposure techniques: Although there are no hard and fast rules for choosing exposure, the following techniques will help you arrive at a reasonable setting:

• Auto-iris is a good starting point. The auto-iris usually produces images containing the full dynamic range of the camera. This is a useful starting point from which variations can be chosen. Keep in mind that most cameras tend to overexpose in auto-iris producing white areas with absolutely no detail. Use auto-iris to find a setting, make adjustments to ensure that no areas of the frame are overexposed, and then turn auto-iris off to avoid iris changes as the scene unfolds.

• Set iris before shooting. Survey the scene and carefully set the iris for the action you anticipate. Do not wait until action is unfolding to make these decisions.

• Use zebras*. Zebras are exposure indicators visible within the viewfinder and are essential for determining exposure. Different manufacturers set these differently, so read the documentation and understand how they work. Zebras are thin diagonal lines that appear in bright areas of the picture. Areas with zebra are nearly white. The operator can assume that anything brighter than the zebra will appear white and possibly over-exposed. In general, most shots should contain some areas with zebra and possible small regions of white, but this will depend on the intent of the director and the dynamics of the scene.

• Use natural breaks in action to make adjustments. The documentary camera operator faces constantly changing situations. There is nothing worse than iris changes in the middle of important action. The way to avoid this is to anticipate action and make iris adjustments during natural breaks where one anticipates edits might occur.

• Avoid over-exposure. Underexposure degrades picture quality, while overexposure can be catastrophic. Over-exposed areas are white and have no detail. This detail cannot be recovered and is forever lost. Under-exposure, however, can be corrected to some degree during post-production. The under-exposed image utilises a smaller portion of the dynamic range of the camera. The image can be recovered by increasing video gain and adjusting black levels. Detail is often lost in dark areas and noise is added, but the results are seldom catastrophic. Given a choice between risking over- and under-exposure, always choose to under-expose.

The documentary camera operator must make difficult choices in dynamic situations and getting the exposure right is one of the most challenging. There are no simple rules for setting exposure; however, it is obvious when the camera operator has not thought about exposure. The results are almost always mediocre.

Focal length

Many students of documentary will have no idea what focal length is. Modern video cameras often have no markings to indicate focal length and the free use of zoom lenses has allowed students to avoid thinking about this important concept. Focal length is the distance between the optical centre of the lens and the imaging plane. A long focal length produces a narrow-angle telescopic image. A short focal length produces a wide-angle image. Focal length is measured in millimetres and the effect of focal length depends on this distance and the size of the imaging plane. Mini-DV cameras have very small imaging sensors and consequently use shorter focal length lenses to achieve similar telephoto or wide-angle effects.

Before the development of zoom lenses, camera operators swapped lenses to achieve specific effects. The 35mm cinematographer might have a collection of lenses beginning at 18mm and ending at 300mm. The choice of lens was dictated by the effect desired. This was an active decision made for aesthetic reasons. It is an exceedingly important decision because it affects the way the image is formed and the relationships between objects in the frame. The significance of focal length is often forgotten by camera operators accustomed to zoom lenses. To understand why, let's look at how different focal lengths affect the image.

Long focal length lenses have a narrow field of view. Subjects that are far away, appear large in the frame. Short focal length lenses have a wide field of view. Subjects that are far away appear very small in the frame. Using this level of understanding, many operators simply adjust the zoom lens (change focal length) until the subject is the right size. This approach completely obscures the importance and power of focal length. Furthermore, many operators choose to shoot using short focal length (wide-angle) because shots appear steadier, do not require tripods, and are easier to frame. These sort of compromises are often necessary but should never be made lightly.

Focal length when combined with camera placement is one of the most powerful tools available to the cinematographer. This combination allows him/her to draw attention to, or obscure elements, in the frame. It gives the camera the power to control the relationships of objects and actors in the scene and to reveal elements in a controlled fashion. It is one of the fundamental keys to creating powerful images.

Assume that the director has asked for a medium shot of a person. The medium shot should encompass the subject's head and their upper body. By experimenting with camera placement, we can see the effect of focal length on the subject. First, put the camera very close, for instance one metre from the subject. At this distance, a medium shot can only be achieved with a short focal length of 9mm. The shot is wide-angle, revealing not only the subject but also much of the room around him. Everything is visible and in focus; windows, shelves, drapes, and whatever else might be in the room. These things may add to a sense of place or may detract from the subject. They may be important or irrelevant. The frame is busy and cluttered.

As the subject talks, gestures, and leans to and from the camera, it becomes apparent that this motion is highly exaggerated. The slightest motion towards the camera makes things look disproportionately large, and movements away disproportionately small. Features on the face look slightly distorted. The nose appears more pronounced than normal.

Next, try placing the camera as far away from the subject as the space will allow. At a distance of 7m, a medium shot can only be achieved using a long focal length of 120mm. This medium shot looks completely different. The subject fills the frame as before, but this time there is very little visible in the background. Objects in front and behind the subject are out of focus. The field of view is very narrow and very little of the room can be seen. Very little can be discerned about the location and all attention rests on the subject. As the subject moves, you notice that forward and backward movements are not pronounced as before and appear to be squashed into a flat plane. In fact, you notice that everything looks a little flat. This shot has less depth.

After the extreme wide angle and extreme long shot, try a range of focal lengths to examine their effect on the subject. The chart (table 1) and photographs (figure 9) overleaf indicate what you might experience.

Focal length and fly-on-the-wall

There are many examples of how focal length affects composition and ultimately the way the shot is perceived. Students of documentary should carefully analyse fiction films because most are shot largely with medium and long focal lengths. Wide shots using short focal lengths are considered a special effect and reserved for scenes where they are appropriate. There are many reasons to avoid wide-angle shots. Medium focal length lenses create a more natural sense of depth. Wide-angle shots create a distorted sense of space which can have unintended effects.

Editing is much easier with medium and long focal length shots. There are less objects and people in the shot and therefore it is easier to match action between shots to create a seamless cut. Cutting from one wide-angle shot to another can be very disturbing.

By using medium and long focal length lenses, the director can control the content of the shots better and limit the amount of extraneous detail. Wide shots tend to be cluttered and busy. They reveal the entire location and often include unnecessary detail. Using longer focal lengths, the director can decide what is important and what should be left out. In documentary production, the longer lens gives the director the ability to exclude detail or limit disclosure. This is very important if the director wishes to draw the viewers' attention away from the environment and towards the subject in the frame.

Titicut Follies provides numerous examples of effective choice of focal lengths. Wiseman never shows us more of the location than is necessary. His camera work concentrates on the face of his actors and never waivers. The few examples where he uses anything other than long focal lengths, he does so with a reason.

There are two scenes that exemplify this technique. Jim, an older inmate, is castigated for not keeping his room tidy by one of the prison guards. The camera follows Jim and his tormentor as he is escorted to the barber for a shave. Throughout the journey, the shave, and the return, the guard keeps asking Jim if he will tidy his

Focal Length	Distance to Subject	Effect	Strengths	Weaknesses
9mm	1.5m	Wide field of view. Depth exaggerated.	Easy to hand-hold. Reveals location.	Difficult to light. Difficult to edit. Confusing, Busy.
15mm	2.0m	Slightly narrower field of view. Changes in depth appear more normal.	Image appears more normal while revealing much of the location.	Same as 9mm.
25mm	2.5m	Features are not distorted at all. Faces and objects seem to have normal shapes.	'Normal' relationships of objects in frame.	Can be boring.
60mm	3.5m	Narrow field of view limits view of background. Depth of field decreases so that background focus is soft. Depth is compressed.	Limits view of background and removes unwanted distractions. Can be flattering for portraits. Easier to light and control.	Difficult to hand-hold. Requires tripod and steady operator. Depth is compressed and may appear unnatural.
120mm	7.0m	Very narrow field of view. Depth compression is pronounced. This has the effect of isolating the viewer from the subject.	Subject is completely isolated from surroundings. Depth of focus is very shallow.	Depth is highly compressed. Impossible to hand-hold. Action is difficult to follow

table 1
**the effects of a range of
focal lengths on photographed subjects**

9mm lens

15mm lens

25mm lens

60mm lens

120mm lens

figure 9
the effect of focal length

room tomorrow. And Jim always responds that he will, but the guard persists, ignoring his replies. The entire scene is shot in close and medium shots revealing the distress on Jim's face. Wiseman is clearly telling us this is torture. When Jim is escorted back to the cell, Wiseman changes focal length to a wide shot. There is nothing in the cell. There is nothing to tidy, there is only Jim and his bare feet pounding the ground. The sudden release from the medium and close shots to the wide shot of this old, naked man in a barren cell is powerful and profound. Had Wiseman revealed the cell before this moment, or had he used wide shots throughout, this final shot would not have had the poignancy that it did.

Wiseman never clutters his shots with unnecessary content. His tight shots with long focal length lenses tell you exactly what he wants to reveal and nothing more. When he does use wide shots he uses them to great effect. In the prison courtyard, Wiseman provides some insight into the mental illness of the inmates. We see one man through a series of close-ups as he rants incessantly about the Vietnam War. He speaks passionately as though there is a large audience hanging on his words. Suddenly, in the background, a second inmate becomes visible. He is standing on his head, singing. The focal length changes to a wide shot showing the first man in the courtyard with no one listening to his tirade. Now the second man is fully revealed. He is standing on his head singing, again, to no one. The wide-angle lens reveals the space, the context, and in this case, the isolation and anguish of these two inmates. The sequence continues with a series of close-ups of the second man singing. Again, this powerful sequence would not have been possible without the judicious use of wide-angle lenses, and Wiseman's passion for disclosing only what he chooses and nothing more.

Choosing the right focal length for each shot is exceedingly important. It is a decision that should be taken with careful consideration for the effect this will have on the scene. Camera operators would be wise not to frame shots through the viewfinder, but rather use a combination of camera placement and focal length to achieve the desired effect.

Camera support

Hand-held footage can be engaging, exciting, and immediate. It has qualities we have come to expect from news broadcasts in war zones. It has the gritty, harsh reality of real life. Used in the right circumstances, the hand-held camera can be very powerful indeed.

Documentary film-makers are often enticed by the immediacy and simplicity of hand-held filming and choose to shoot everything hand-held for all the wrong reasons. The result is unbridled mediocrity that is at least disappointing and at worst annoying. Hand-held cinematography is one technique for camera support. Like all techniques, it should be used consciously with intent and understanding. It should not be used because the operator is too lazy to carry and set up the tripod.

As with all techniques, hand-held cinematography works best when mixed with others, such as steady tripod shots. Hand-held shots can add confusion, immediacy, and tension. Used all the time, it becomes clearly visible as mediocre camera work.

The tripod shot should form the core of all production. Always use a tripod unless there is good reason such as: confusion, tension, and immediacy are appropriate to the subject; the camera must move quickly between set-ups; there is genuinely insufficient time to set up a tripod (it takes a skilled operator no more than ten seconds to set and level a tripod).

The Tripod should be considered an essential tool for all locations. Choosing not to use a tripod should always be an active decision with a full understanding of the effect on the viewers.

Camera movement

One of the hallmarks of high-quality production is camera movement. Documentary film-makers often assume that camera movement (other than hand-held) is impossible in real-world situations. This is simply not true. It is perfectly reasonable to set up a dolly and track for documentary production. For instance, if you know that action will occur at a table, a semicircular track gives the operator immediate access to set-ups at every angle. Camera movement can inject a dynamic element in an otherwise dry and boring scene. Dolly shots can be used in documentary production, but they are difficult to achieve and can be costly. Framing shots dynamically during dollies can be difficult and requires considerable practice and experience; however, the effect can be spectacular.

Camera movement can also be achieved using camera stabilisation. In the hands of experienced operators, stabilisation rigs such as Steadicam can achieve fluid motion in difficult circumstances. There are also inexpensive versions for mini-digital cameras.

LIGHTING

Approaches to lighting

In the early days of television, engineers would walk around the set holding a light meter to determine if there was sufficient illumination to make a picture. Illumination is what we see at a football match. News reporters often illuminate their subjects with a light mounted on the camera. Lighting and illumination are entirely different things. Lighting is less about illuminating the scene and more about casting shadows. Shadows give shape to objects and create textures. Shadows create moods and feeling. Shadows create richness, depth, and reveal meaning. Illumination is for football, surgeons, and dentists, not for film-making.

Lighting is as important to documentary as it is to high-budget drama. The documentary director may have less control, but by combining exposure, camera placement, and a few carefully placed lighting instruments, the documentary film-maker can achieved powerful results. There are many approaches to lighting, described here in three broad strokes:

Full lighting: the most powerful option is to control all light sources. This is most often the case in high-budget cinematography where every source of light and every reflection is carefully controlled. Available light is seldom used, and where it is applied, it is filtered, balanced, and directed. Documentary film-makers seldom light to this extent although there are notable exceptions. *The Thin Blue Line* employs dramatic reconstruction of a crime scene. Here the scenes are artificially lit to achieve drama and suspense. In most situations, however, documentary film-makers usually rely on available light or some combination of available and artificial light.

Partial lighting: documentary film-makers must work in a broad range of lighting conditions with neither the budget nor the desire to replace all ambient light. The best solution is to use light that is available and augment it with carefully placed instruments. These instruments should be chosen and placed to cast shadows and create textures.

Available light: this alone can be unacceptable for many reasons. Offices are typically lit with overhead fluorescent lights. These lights provide good illumination for working but create shadowy faces and soft, bland light across the scene. Surfaces are brightly lit and faces remain dark. Direct overhead lighting creates poor results. Some locations feature large windows. Windows can provide good sources of light that casts interesting shadows; however, they can be difficult to control. If windows appear in the shots, it can be difficult to balance exposure. Industrial sites often use mercury vapour or sodium lights that are difficult to balance and produce undesired tonal values. All of these problems can be ameliorated to some degree using additional lighting.

There is insufficient space here to explore the tools and techniques of lighting except to offer a few suggestions. Firstly, examine the available light and try to understand why it is inadequate. Once the problems are clear, it is easier to craft a solution. In an office, the lighting is typically flat and overhead. This can be remedied with two small instruments. One to cast shadows across the face of the subject. This helps bring out contours, shapes, and textures. Another light from behind or the side can separate the subject from the background by providing a soft highlight around the edges. Simple two-point lighting can help lift a scene and give it clarity, depth, and shape, resulting in a more engaging image.

In some locations you may find that there are too many lights. Turning off some overhead lights, opening blinds, and adding a couple of instruments may create new shadows and new effects.

Balancing colour temperature

Students of documentary production often have difficulty understanding and manipulating colour balance. This is because the human eye is highly adaptable, adjusting easily to changes in light. We see well under a broad range of light from the Mediterranean sun to low-pressure sodium lights on the motorway. The camera is not as adaptable and is especially unforgiving where there are mixed light sources.

Domestic lighting is always a problem. Houses are lit with low colour temperature incandescent light bulbs. These are often mixed with high temperature daylight from windows and fluorescent light in kitchens. Low temperature lights are orange in tone, daylight is pale blue, and fluorescent tends to appear green. The eye quickly compensates for these changes, but the camera does not. Filming in these locations can be a nightmare. Often the only solution is to eliminate all but one source and add a few instruments to match.

This quality of light is usually described by colour temperature. A black box heated to 3200° Kelvin would radiate a light of the same tonal value as a tungsten lighting instrument. Spotlights used at home have a colour temperature of about 2900° Kelvin and therefore appear more orange. Daylight varies between 5900 and 6500° Kelvin and appears more blue. Other light sources such as fluorescent and sodium do not produce light in the same way. These lights emit what is called a discontinuous spectrum of light. They emit light in various colours which, when combined, appear white. These discontinuous spectrum lights produce unexpected results in video and film.

Adjusting colour balance begins at the camera. Using an appropriate white card, place the card so that it is well illuminated by the primary light source, aim the camera at the card, filling the frame, and then record the white balance. The camera simply adjusts the signals from the red, blue and green chips to produce a white signal from the reflected light. This will provide satisfactory colour under most lighting situations. Difficulties arise when there is more than one light source. For instance, offices are often lit with fluorescent light and daylight. Colour balance can be further complicated with the addition of incandescent light to augment available light. In this situation the light from the incandescent light must be filtered to approximate the primary light source.

A broad range of gel filters are available for use in video and film production. These come in sheets and rolls in a wide variety of tones and shades. Every lighting kit should have at least the following gels:

Full Blue: converts tungsten incandescent light to daylight by removing red light.

Half-Blue: cools incandescent light to so that the difference between daylight and light from the instruments is not as pronounced. Half-blue is very useful for lighting in rooms with large windows. The filtered incandescent light appears warmer than daylight creating a gentle colour contrast between exterior and interior light sources.

85 filter gel: this orange gel is used to convert daylight into incandescent light of 3200° Kelvin by removing blue. It is most often used to lower the colour temperature of HMI lights used in combination with incandescent lights. It is also used to cover windows to match light coming in the windows to light from incandescent instruments.

Fluorescent Green: fluorescent lights vary greatly depending on manufacturer and model. Matching incandescent lights with fluorescent can be difficult. Good results can be achieved using an assortment of light-green filters combined with half-blue and placed over incandescent lights. The resulting light from the incandescent instruments matches the fluorescent lights reasonably well. The best approach is to have a selection of filters on hand and experiment until the best results are achieved.

Even carefully matched light sources will vary in tonal quality. For this reason, the camera must be carefully white-balanced to the primary light source. If the scene is primarily lit by fluorescent light, carefully position the white card so that it reflects as much fluorescent light as possible. If the primary source is filtered incandescent, place the card so that it is broadly illuminated by this light source. I have found that attempting to white balance from mixed sources produces poor results. Neither the primary light source nor the secondary sources are properly balanced and the results can be unsettling.

Finally, colour balance can be used creatively to great effect. There is no reason to adjust the camera to every change in light quality. The content and purpose of the film may benefit from changes in tonal qualities. Golden light at dusk may be an important element in the scene. A white balance in this location would create a scene with white light from the sun and a dark blue sky – perhaps not what the director intended. Similarly, a dark, overcast day will create a cold blue effect when shot using daylight pre-sets. The creative camera operator can go beyond the realm of colour balance to use filters before the lens or filters during white balance to create other effects or tonal values. Colour balance is another important tool. It is a setting that is often made passively without active consideration of the consequences or the potential for aesthetic effect.

Making the best of available light

There will always be some situations where it is impossible to augment available lighting and the director has no option but to use the light that is available even though it is of mixed colour values. Even in these difficult situations, there is still a great deal that can be done to improve the quality of shots through careful placement of the camera and/or the subject.

One of the most difficult lighting situations is in long, dimly lit hallways. Imagine fluorescent lights placed at five-metre intervals against white walls. Faces are in shadow and bodies appear dark against the white walls. Acceptable results can be achieved by placing the subject between two lights and facing at a 40 degree angle away from the light. If you look carefully at the way the light falls, it is possible to place the subject so that the overhead lights cast interesting shadows across the face while illuminating the eyes. The light behind the subject provides a little 'rim-lighting' to separate the subject from the background. Finally, place the camera at some distance on a tripod and use a long focal length to minimise the prominence of the background. By carefully placing the camera, one can choose a darker portion of the background to ensure the foreground appears slightly brighter and more prominent.

Careful choice of camera and subject placement can be very effective in a wide variety of situations. Perhaps you are filming a telephone conversation in an office. Must it happen at your subject's desk? Perhaps it would be better by the window? Perhaps the camera could be placed across the room so that the subject's face is lit by strong, soft light from the side while the bulk of the face remains in shadow. The possibilities are limitless once you see every light source as something that can be controlled and manipulated through careful placement of the camera and subject.

A JOURNEY OF COMPROMISE

Film-making encompasses many diverse genres. What is shared across this diversity, and perhaps all art, is a desire to evoke a response in the viewer. The power of a film to evoke rests on the ability of the film-maker to articulate the language of film effectively. This requires creativity, imagination, and a great deal of technical understanding.

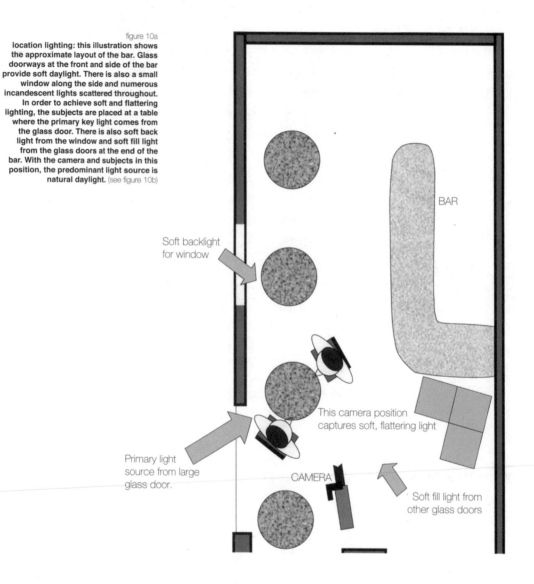

figure 10a
location lighting: this illustration shows the approximate layout of the bar. Glass doorways at the front and side of the bar provide soft daylight. There is also a small window along the side and numerous incandescent lights scattered throughout. In order to achieve soft and flattering lighting, the subjects are placed at a table where the primary key light comes from the glass door. There is also soft back light from the window and soft fill light from the glass doors at the end of the bar. With the camera and subjects in this position, the predominant light source is natural daylight. (see figure 10b)

BAR

Soft backlight
for window

This camera position
captures soft, flattering light

Primary light
source from large
glass door.

CAMERA

Soft fill light from
other glass doors

figure 10b
location lighting

Good film-making is informed by a broad understanding of production techniques without regard to genre. The fiction film-maker must understand the subtle nuances of documentary film while the documentary film-maker must know how to craft and structure images with the precision of a dramatic film, as is witnessed in the documentary work of Frederick Wiseman. The well-informed film-maker draws upon the entire vocabulary of the language and not just the clichés and conventions of one genre: witness the documentary styles used in *Gladiator* and the dramatic techniques employed in *The Thin Blue Line*. *Titicut Follies* and *The Thin Blue Line* employ the technique of selective disclosure. This technique, most often associated with dramatic films, allows the director powerful influence over the scene. The well-informed and experienced film-maker will draw upon his/her knowledge of a broad range of production techniques to craft effective images, regardless of the genre.

I often describe the film-making process as one of constant compromise. The documentary film-maker begins with a brilliant idea, a vision, an inspired view of the truth. At each stage of the production process, this brilliant vision is, in some small way, compromised. There is never enough money or sufficient time; shots are seldom as good as we imagined; lighting did not match the action; camera placement was off the mark; exposure was slightly off; sound is not as clear as it should be. At each stage, the director must make choices and compromises, and with each decision, the director takes a small step backwards from the inspired vision that began the process. In this sense, film-making is a journey and the objective is to arrive at the destination with as much of the original vision as possible. The greater your understanding of production techniques, the greater the chance that the original vision makes it through to the end. Quality in all phases of production, not just camera work, will ensure that our images are evocative and our audiences realise the greater truths we seek to reveal.

FURTHER READING

Grant, B. K. & J. Sloniowski (eds) (1998) *Documenting the Documentary*. Detroit: Wayne State University Press.

Katz, S. (1991) *Shot by Shot*. Studio City, CA: Michael Wiese Productions.

Rabinger, M. (1998) *Directing the Documentary*, 3rd edn. Boston: Focal Press.

Rosenthal, A. (1996) *Writing, Directing and Producing Documentary Films and Videos*, 2nd edn. Carbondale: Southern Illinois University Press.

Fielding, R. (1969) *The Focal Encyclopaedia of Film and TV Techniques*. New York: Hastings House.

USEFUL WEBSITE

www.chicagomediaworks.com/2instructworks/3editing_doccinematography.htm

06 **creative sound** ron geesin

Sound is for hearing. Obvious? But consider the number and forms of sounds you try not to hear and the amount of energy used avoiding those niggling nuisances of unwanted hums, barks, crashes, whines, clatters and buzzes of other people's lives and systems, reminding you that everyone's scurrying about, clamouring for a crust. This chapter is a gentle immersion in sound, following the principle that the only way to 'know' about something is to be there. To swim in water, you have to get into it first. So, we are going into the vast swimming pool of sound, first feeling the water, then getting in, then floating, then swimming, then practising and perfecting particular strokes. Somewhere in there is underwater swimming too.

From 'feeling' to 'floating' in the above analogy, I mean learning about that most complex and deep of the sensory experiences, the medium of sound. When you get to the 'swimming' stage you are into the main subject: the applications of creative, organised sound in the documentary-film medium. The water analogy is particularly apt because if you do not understand it and react in sympathy with it, you're dead! Usually, you do have the choice of staying out of water but you cannot stay out of sound since it usually carries at least half the total message and accounts for a major part of customer attention in a documentary film, so it is wise to learn a lot about it.

Since sound is often received and dealt with on many subconscious levels, it is difficult to use words to do it any kind of justice. Much of the best sound structuring ('composition') is achieved by disengaging the conscious analytical mind and letting the subconscious bubble up and flow free – and you will spend a lifetime practising and doing it. There is a lot of common sense involved, and you will get a long way by listening and asking questions, like:

- how does a bird sing two notes at once?
- why is an obvious beat needed in popular music?
- how does a composer, Elgar for instance, get such emotion across?
- why does the sound of 'fingernails down a blackboard' annoy so much?
- why is most people's favourite soothing sound the sea washing across pebbles?
- why is music so important in our lives?

Sound in documentary film, or in any other situation for that matter, is creative. You find it however you can, and you use it wherever you can. These statements open a big debate about whether you are portraying what you observe as the surface of a subject, because that is what you see and hear, or something of the inner workings, the spirit or soul. If you lean at all towards the latter, you need creative sound to literally 'get into' and project the subject. You also need it to help fill in the missing senses, smell, taste and touch and to augment the dimensions of the picture, actually and metaphorically.

The best conversations are recorded when the participants are unaware you are recording, however you achieve that. Many sounds cannot be got 'in the wild', so you make them in the studio. Seemingly wrong sounds are often right. A composition by a Nazi-sympathiser might be just right for that concentration-camp survivor. Stimuli from other sensory media can be inspiring: a documentary about the early French film-maker Abel Gance used material shot by his cameraman; one scene showed a self-winding camera whizzing down a thin rope to achieve an eye-watering zoom right into a character's face. This visual trick affected my attitude to creative sound-making. Ingenuity is the key.

SOUND IN LIFE

What is it?

Sound is normally accepted to be vibrations, usually transmitted through air to our ears, between the frequency limits of human hearing, about 15Hz[1] at the low, or bass, end and 20KHz[2] at the high, or treble, end. It does not travel in a vacuum, but can travel through gases, liquids and solids. In the case of vibrations in air, they travel in a 'knock-on' pressure way, that is to say that the air molecules move forward and back, more or less stationary, imparting that positive and negative pressure energy oscillation to their neighbours until the energy spreads out and is used up or spent. It does not travel in the wave pattern so often illustrated in physics books and seen on an oscilloscope screen. That is in fact a graph in time of the positive and negative pressure movements. Interestingly, though, if you transmit sound through water, positioning the sound activator – a waterproof speaker for example – near the surface, you will see some of the 'waves' seemingly travel across the surface. These are delayed, slow-motion pressure reactions of the water to some of the lower frequencies. The most sensitive frequency region of the human ear is between about 1KHz and 2KHz, which is roughly between one and two octaves above Middle C on a keyboard (C4-C5 in MIDI) or upwards from the 8th fret on the top E guitar string. Not surprisingly, this is also the frequency region that carries most of the defining frequencies in the human speaking voice and why telephone sound peaks in this area. High frequencies are more directional but travel less far than low frequencies.

Sound comes from two theoretical extremes: single oscillations which, in their pure form, can only be generated from electronic equipment; and noise (the sum of all frequencies). In 'real' life, you can approximate a single oscillation by singing 'Ooo' with a rounded mouth, and noise by going 'Sshhh....' loudly, or you can hear this from a television when the transmitting station is off-air, or a channel is detuned. The frequency components of all sounds can be identified somewhere between these extremes.[3] Added to these are:

- *dynamics*: the amount of loudness ('volume' or 'level') and its variation within any event.
- *tone**: quite often called 'timbre', the particular combination of frequencies that make anything from a smooth to a rough texture together with their variation within the tone.
- *time*: the length of any event and the time taken (possibly by silence) between events.

We tend to separate sound into 'unwanted' and 'wanted'. Unwanted sound is usually called 'noise' (or racket, row, hubbub, mess, etc). To purge ourselves of the sound products of technology, like building sites, escalators, cars, motorbikes and washing machines, we travel to the seaside to be literally washed by the soothing sound of sea splashing or trickling over sand and pebbles or, if inland, sitting by some kind of flowing water. Absurdly, we are now buying these soothing sounds on recordings made by the technology we are trying to escape from.

John Cage, the American composer, philosopher and humorist, wrote in 1937:

Wherever we are, what we hear is mostly noise. When we ignore it, it disturbs us. When we listen to it, we find it fascinating. The sound of a truck at fifty miles per hour. Static between the stations. Rain. We want to capture and control these sounds ... we can compose and perform a quartet for explosive motor, wind, heartbeat, and landslide. (Cage 1968: 3)

What does it do?

Of all sensory experiences, sound is the most complex. There are many quotations from great writers and thinkers throughout the history of writing. Here are a few key ones:

- 'Noise, n. A stench in the ear. Undomesticated music. The chief product and authenticating sign of civilisation.' Ambrose Bierce
- 'Many an irksome noise, when a long way off, is heard as music.' Henry Thoreau
- 'Silence is the mother of truth.' Benjamin Disraeli

Maybe it is because we cannot normally see, touch, feel, taste or smell sound that it is harder to understand. Why should we want to? Well, that is for another book but it seems that the industrial, technological society that we have all built around us as a supposed improvement to the quality of life has, by its very nature, suppressed our appreciation of the deeper, more spiritual aspects of sound and music (see Shafer 1977; Berendt 1988, 1991; Toop 1995). So, most of us attempt to translate this deep, multi-levelled emotional medium into words and pictures. Just notice how often, when you meet musicians or composers, do you ask, 'What kind of music do you make?' rather than knowing and accepting that their best role in society is to communicate their emotions in their own style, stir up or affect your emotions, and generally be part of the true enjoyment of life. If you examine the attitudes to, and roles of, musicians in the older, (sometimes) more spiritually-minded cultures of India and Africa, they might work within a broad and loose musical category, but nothing like the tight definitions we attempt for 'techno', 'house', 'punk jazz', 'folk rock' and 'handbag grunge'(!). They are religious (in the best spiritual sense) gurus, possessors and seekers of wisdom, continually searching within their music structures by means of inspired improvisation for more meaningful representations of life's joys and sorrows.

The other, more physical, property of sound is that it leaks! It invades your physical and mental space by crawling under doors, vibrating through closed windows, travelling through walls and floors and, if you do not want it at that moment, generally driving you potty! This means that, on the one hand, your fellow beings can signal to you, remind or warn you of an approaching event and, on the other hand, drive you to near murder by:

- playing a hated style of music loudly in the next room
- slamming car doors at 3am in a reverberant street
- holding you forever on the phone with 'suitable' music
- sandpapering your ears with mobile phone call-signals
- keeping a yapping dog in a nearby courtyard

You can realise from this that, if you are going to use sound as part of your expressive observations of the diverse activities of fellow humans, you must learn a lot about it by continually noticing what it does and how it affects you.

Where is it from?

Since sound has to be transmitted from somewhere, we need to identify the sources. These are, broadly:

- human
- nature
- machine

Maybe 'machine' is a product of human and nature. Certainly, music is one specialised product of human and machine. I propose that, if you can learn all about the sounds emitted from the human body, internally and externally, you will be well on the way to understanding about most sound. You do not need technology in the form of microphones, amplifiers, oscilloscopes, computers and loudspeakers for this. In fact, you do not even need a musical instrument[4] and could spend (probably 'are spending') a lifetime studying and interpreting the sounds made by the human animal: languages, interjections, cries and songs.

The world of nature provides us with a multi-coloured palette of possibilities:

• the elements

• plants

• animals

Elemental sounds are fascinating, from the many different tone textures of wind to a stone bouncing down a cliff. I know plants do not make many sounds, certainly not loud ones, unless they are being acted upon by other forces, or falling over, but a study of the different sounds of wind and the intricacies of birdsong will give you many ideas. The more you slow down blackbird song to study it, the more complex it becomes! The sounds of animals are forever fascinating and there are many recordings to prove it, but we cannot always get close enough to an animal to hear any sound at all. Many wildlife sounds in documentaries used to be made by a mother and daughter team in a studio full of gravel, twigs, containers of water and their mouths: consider the wet click of a lizard's tongue catching a fly, or a lion dismembering its prey. This process of watching a moving picture and making appropriate sounds by whatever means is called 'Foley' work*, after an American of the same name.

Machines have saturated our world with sound – and we invented them. Many of them can permanently damage your hearing:

• weaving looms, particularly nineteenth-century ones

• jet engines

• loudspeakers in clubs and concerts

The quiet vacuum cleaner was designed early in the twentieth century, but users thought it was not working properly so it was re-noised. The quiet typewriter was rejected by bosses who could not hear if the typists were working. My computer printer plays a complete musical work when first switched on. It was not designed to do that, but I perceive the whirrs and clicks of cartridge-priming that way. Musical instruments are machines, extensions of our hands and voices, and are diverse and wonderful. What magic can be extracted from a bamboo tube with a few holes burned in it![5] From an ocarina to a contrabass bassoon, from an 'mbira' (African thumb piano) to a concert grand piano, even including the recording machine and computer – all are tools for expression, if we can organise and discipline ourselves to 'speak' through them. Some hard work, often of the best and most enjoyable kind, has to be done.

How do we get it?

This is a good example of balancing book learning with doing: do some, read some.

First, you should have some idea of what you want. This is because our very sophisticated ability to filter sounds in our heads becomes a disadvantage when we go out with recording equipment. Just study how good you are at focusing on someone talking in a crowded room, not necessarily someone near to you. You can even be talking to someone near to you and listening to someone two metres behind you. This is psychoacoustic filtering, but the microphone cannot do that. Also, in a live situation, your brain fills in some of the defining high frequencies that are missing in transmission: the sound may be coming from another room, or is masked by wind noise, or someone is talking with their head turned away, or with hand over mouth.

So, to collect sounds in our heads, all we need is an ear well-connected to a brain, but to store, reconstruct or combine them in new ways and project them back into the environment, we need recording, editing, mixing and playback equipment. From the early part of the twentieth century, when recording equipment took up the space of a car, to the twenty-first century, when many times higher quality sound is recorded on something the size of a small bar of chocolate, recordists have been out there, waiting for a week in a wood for a small bird, freezing solid to get a glacier cracking, curled up sweating under a stage to capture a particularly fine theatrical or musical performance or risking their whole hearing system high up in a tower to preserve something of the strange world of bell-ringing. Every situation is a learning experience.

To record sound, the questions have to be:

- where is it coming from?
- what are its components?
- do you want all or part of it?
- what microphone (or other vibration route) is best used?
- what is the best microphone position: a) for clear sound; b) for the camera?
- will a processor (limiter, expander, etc) be necessary?

For answers to technical questions, refer to some of the many books on sound recording equipment and techniques.[6] I am going to go through some fundamental points together with hints and tips, and always remember that, while most of the equipment and techniques are attempting electromechanically to do what we do naturally with our ears and brain, we need to concentrate on guiding them by really listening.

Microphones

All microphones are transducers: they convert energy from one form to another, in this case from air and surface vibrations to electrical oscillations. Use them and learn. Move them about, listening carefully on good quality headphones for the different characteristics and effects. For our purposes, the main categories are:

- hand-held/stand alone – many different sensitivity fields and responses
- pressure zone
- tie or lapel
- contact

The first, and very broad, category contains those most often called 'microphones' (mics), of which there are several types like 'dynamic', 'ribbon', and 'condenser'. Within these types, there are several specialist designs. Some look like large bottles, specifically for soundproof studios. Some are for close vocal work on stage and others, usually seen at sports events and clad like giant furry caterpillars, are 'rifle' or 'shotgun' mics, specifically designed to focus on a subject and minimise the pickup of any sound outside the 'beam'. The mic part is a long tube of 20mm diameter and the furry coat is a windshield to reduce wind blast. Some mics have switches to partially reject heavy bass before it gets a chance to overload any part of the recorder circuit, causing distorted sound. Often, the ideal mic for a particular situation is not available to you so you have to improvise. If you have to close-record a breathy voice with a standard good quality 'hand-held' mic, position its head slightly to the side of the subject's mouth, not straight on. This still picks up those necessary high frequencies, but allows the worst 'plosives' (which create pops and explosions) freely past the sensitive diaphragm. If not experienced, your subject usually turns to face the mic – you must aim them at some other target. Alternatively, you can make a 'pop screen': one or two layers of old nylon stocking stretched across a wire hoop positioned between mic and mouth. Outdoor wind noise is a big problem – try various windshields in combination with a sheltered position, or wait. Concentrate on checking that there is not a distant squawking chicken or humming aeroplane – very difficult to eliminate later.

Creative microphone techniques are useful. While some anticipate 'processing', other effects can be got only at the microphone stage,[7] and it is best to take the natural raw sound on one channel and the altered one on another:

- fast tracking – following the subject (watch for wind generation)
- swirling (development of above)
- acoustic modulation (e.g. cardboard tube on end, or bucket mute)
- intentional muffling

Pressure zone mics really belong to the first category, but they look very different: a little raised bump of a sensor mounted on a square flat metal plate. They are very good at picking up everything coming at them, 180° all round one side of the plate, and if placed on a table are not particularly noticed by a camera.

You have seen 'tie' or 'lapel'[8] mics, probably on television. Again, they really belong to the first category but are in for some special treatment here. They are high-quality devices, designed to maximise on the high-frequency components of speech, but I remind you that high frequencies are more directional than low frequencies and, in the case of the human mouth and chin, the worst place to pick up these defining frequencies is on the tie or lapel! True, there are times when a talking subject is running or jumping about and the only way is to wire them up and transmit the result by radio. This is a 'radio mic', in fact an ordinary mic plugged into a radio transmitter. In their zeal to please the camera-person and/or director, some recordists further muffle the high frequencies by fixing the mic behind a scarf or other fabric. Use a rifle mic wherever possible, or any other tricks you learn, and fall back on the 'lapel' approach only when stumped. If the subject is not moving much, a lapel mic hidden in flowers on a table or in a desk accessory tray could be tried.

Contact mics/transducers are very interesting. The older ones were sometimes bulky and contained a magnet as part of their functioning. Modern ones are often 'piezo-electric' – a crystal structure emitting a lot of electrical energy when vibrated. I used to adapt 1960s gramophone pickup cartridges but now there is a magical material called piezo film – a little thicker than baking foil which, when manufactured in a wafer strip,[9] can be stuck onto a surface to reveal a whole world of internal sounds[10] – no good for air-borne sounds though. It has to go through a special pre-amplifier before the recorder. Some time ago, I worked on a documentary called the *The Painter and the Pest* (Bandung Productions for Channel 4, 1985) about a then recently-discovered abstract expressionist painter living in New York[11] and wanted to get into the canvas to get that crunchy brush swish that would project what the painter was hearing. I gave the sound recordist one of these transducers and the result was wonderful.

There is another kind of mic technique, 'human technique, with mic'. When interviewing, design questions that draw the best out of the subject. Not: 'Would you say then that cheese is made from milk?' to which you would very likely get, 'Yes!' You could try: 'How do you make cheese?' Do not make appreciative grunts, dueting with the interviewee, as in normal conversation – you cannot edit these out later. Reserve them for obvious pauses, where you can edit, but smile and nod in visual appreciation – this needs some practice. It is very possible to make a documentary about an individual by asking increasingly probing questions in a slightly seductive manner, possibly alternated with an aggressive manner. What the camera and mic gets is that subject gradually being cornered, truly 'stitched up'. The 'creative sound' here is in the interviewer's voice and in those tiny but crucial shakes and hesitancies in the interviewee's voice. Whether the subject ever signs the release form is another matter.

In 1993, I made an impressionistic radio documentary called *Splashpast* (BBC R4, 1993) about a journey down the river Trent.[12] A friend knew a local man with a wonderful accent and a great talent for spontaneous storytelling whose life was entirely connected to the river. I guessed he would not respond well to any kind of questioning and would clam up when he knew the mic was on, so I rigged the environment with two mics and switched on before he arrived. Since he had not seen my friend for ages, he sat down and poured out the story of his previous six months' adventures. Later, I asked him some questions. In the final work, I used a great deal of his vivid story and no answers to questions. He had consented to our using whatever was recorded, but had not asked exactly what. In the media world, there is a kind of willing balance or contract between members of the public pursuing, maybe satisfying, their fantasy to 'get on radio/television', not realising the long-term consequences, and the media saying, 'Thank you very much'.

Recorders

Technology is changing so fast that I can only say, 'Go out and use the best'. The heated discussion between digital and analogue rages continually. Some earlier analogue ¼" tape recorders[13] are still fine machines but bulky, and you have to have some extra studio equipment for editing and processing, or transfer the wanted material to a digital medium. The same is true for the better audio cassette machines.

Many micro digital recorders have a switch marked something like 'AGC' or 'ALC'.[14] This brings in a coarse limiter that senses extra-loud energy and reduces it, along with everything else at that point. You can hear this as a kind of surging and pumping. Unless you are in an emergency situation, or in a steel works where there are unpredictable clangs, or half-traumatised reporting on an air crash, do not use it. Learn to adjust the recording level in conjunction with mic position and ear (headphones). Take notes of what, where, and when to store with the recording, and label everything, even if you are not happy with the result at that time.

AUDIO POST-PRODUCTION

Editing

What used to be done on ¼" tape with an editing block and razor blade, or on a film splicer, is often done digitally now on one of the many computer editing programmes.

When editing a voice track, include the little mouth noises before and after speech – they are more natural – unless you need to eliminate clicky false teeth or a stutter. When constructing tracks for later mixing, do not cut too tight either, unless you want an impact. It leaves you the opportunity to ease into, or gently introduce, the background ambience, and to slide out at the end. Film sound recordists often take a 'buzz' (ambient) track when the rest of the crew have gone to lunch. In the mix, this helps to mask entries of speech that may include unavoidable background noises. Whatever the medium, a clean and methodical technique works better. A film splicer plastered with adhesive tape offcuts does not cut well. A badly labelled sound offcut in a computer program cannot be found again.

Processing

This means altering the raw sound material in some way by controlling or adding:

- pitch (pitch-shifting)
- level (limiting, compressing, expanding, gating)
- tone (filtering, equalising)
- time (time-shifting)
- space (echo, reverberation)
- modulation (inner- or outer-worldy sounds)

Before digital manipulation, if you changed the pitch of a sound on a disc turntable or tape, you changed the speed.[15] Now you can alter either of these independently, within certain limits. If you want to impart the feeling that someone is frightened by a situation, say a train journey, just raising the pitch of the train sound a little can do a lot, because one might perceive things as sounding higher and faster when one's nerves are a-jangle.

Level control is sometimes absolutely necessary: maybe the ratio of high volume to low is simply too great for the medium and the sound-projection system, or you need some other sound in the background which would mask the low volume part, so you experiment with settings in a limiter or compressor (often in the same unit). Watch singers with a hand-held mic: when they know that a certain pitch-region in their voice is louder than another region, they pull the mic away from the mouth, narrowing that volume ratio. Conversely, you might want to heighten the rhythmic components of a machine: you would use an expander to increase the higher level elements and decrease the lower. A more extreme form of this is 'gating' where the low level material is simply shut off.

Tone control is very useful. Although usually called 'equalising', true to this upside-down world of sound, it is better thought of as 'un-equalising'. Suppose you are building a composite track, mixing the elements of speech, music and a low-pitch rumble, maybe from a hospital trolley. Rather than crudely adjusting the relative levels, you could try reducing the bass content of speech, reducing the treble content of the music and increasing the bass content of the rumble. This allows each component its best frequency range, in this particular mix. Messing about with the frequency content of music is most contentious but I have sometimes suggested reducing some of the higher frequencies in my music in a mix where the alternative would have had the music so low that it was wasted.

With digital technology, time control is a powerful addition to the toolbox in fitting a section of sound to a finished picture, or for heightening (more fiddling!) the delivery of a voice-over, maybe even speaking faster than the human mouth can go, without changing pitch.

Echo, usually 'repeat echo' is much used as a device to depict something going wrong in a subject's head (inner space). Its complex form 'reverb'[16] is even more used as an indicator of external spatial volume, or of internal thought reflections or shifts in time.

Modulation is the most contentious sound treatment in the documentary medium because it signals that the sound's gone entirely into the inner, subjective, world, unless you are just modifying a particular reverberation to simulate a narrow tunnel. In certain instances, selected use of processes like phasing/flanging, vocoding and ring modulating may be the only way you can project to an audience either what you think is going on in a subject's head or what you know you have received from the subject in intimate conversation: your interpretation or synthesis of the pitch, tone and timing of delivery of words, minute eye-movements and the changing and positioning of limbs and fingers.

figure 11
sound junction

It may well be that electronic processing in audio evolved from the human desire to express something of the complex multi-dimensions of thoughts and feelings we all get in response to any outside stimulus.

Mixing

In the larger studios, this process is conducted on a 'desk' which slopes and on which it is difficult to rest things because of the faders, or a 'console', where the only person you console is yourself. There are two extremes of mixing, controlled by the 'one' or the 'all'. The process is like a composite orchestra and conductor with a superb expressive result as the goal, but too often tension, panic, a lack of real sound awareness and the sieve of conflicting vested interests creates a mess. The image of a fat film executive coughing on an even fatter cigar at the back of the dubbing studio and spitting, 'My wife doesn't like squeaky sounds like that!' haunts me still. If you cannot spend a year or so at a specialist college to learn this mysterious art, the next best thing is simply to do it. You will soon find out about 'subtractive' and 'additive' techniques: what to leave out and what to fill in.

SOUND SOURCES

You have learnt something about the many sources in life itself, but there are others:

- composers
- production music libraries
- effects libraries
- commercial recordings
- radio/television
- the Net

I have to deal with the subject of composers later. Unlike the found sounds in life, material from the others probably has owners and/or copyright holders. If you are at all in doubt, find out who the interested parties are and clear it.[17] There is usually copyright in:

- the musical work (composition)
- the sound recording
- the performance

Production music libraries have been in business since the start of sound films. They get composers to create a collection of material in the many accepted musical styles, record them and offer the pieces for lease to the media industry. The composer is paid when the work is used commercially by royalties routed through the several collection agencies.[18] Obvious heavy users are given recordings for reference. Others have to go to the 'library', or Net representation, get advice and listen to selections. Either way, you pay by the metre at certain standard rates. A stage further is non-copyright music where the fee paid covers all expected use, the copyright having previously been 'bought out' from the composer. Effects libraries and commercially-issued collections of effects are managed in similar fashion.

If you want to use a commercial recording by a named artist, the situation is different because the performance of the artist is involved in addition to copyright fees. Sometimes the fee asked is prohibitive – but try. Sampling, in the sense of digitally recording a fragment and using it in a mix or composition, is another complication but is also negotiable. If you process or distort a famous artist's performance, you may be sued for copyright infringement and misrepresentation. Technically, if you take any sound off the radio or television and use it commercially, you are infringing copyright, but it is your risk whether they ever find you.

Some parts of all of the above can be found on the Net, and many commercial organisations are working feverishly to develop new ways of protecting copyright.

SOUND IN DOCUMENTARY

The very origin of the term 'document' – proof of action or possession carried on a flat sheet of paper – has, to some extent, held the documentary-film medium down. It is freeing up now as the realisation spreads that there is often more reality inside people's heads than outside.

Through your reading of earlier chapters in this book, you should have some idea of your approach to documentary style which will directly influence your sound treatment. By now, you will be aware that just about anything is possible in the sound half of a film. Also, as a general comment, anyone who is interested in a subject is compelled to research previous examples, in our case through television listings or booking some sessions at the British Film Institute (BFI). Many colleges maintain video libraries which collect relevant material and loan it to students. Look for techniques of timing and dynamics: how real climaxes are built up; how much silence can be held before or after an event; what value there is in a single melodic line. You could even take an existing documentary and replace all sound as an exercise.

It is one thing to analyse previous documentary work and it is another to make something new. Style-language is constantly changing to interact with the current fashion. I say 'interact' because you always have the choice to go with or against that fashion, or make something entirely in your own style to the best, most considered form you can manage.

One of my most successful offerings, both structurally and commercially, was for *Sam Smith – Genuine England* (Arts Council Films, 1976), a twenty-minute documentary on the work of a wood-sculptor.[19] I had just emerged from a terrible experience of a documentary made by mistrusting maniacs and was in no mood for compromise when the director came to me with a finished cut of the film, mute with some sync voice sections. Firstly, a finished cut can be the most awkward to work on because the moment you put some sound on it the perception of internal proportions in the whole work is changed. Secondly, some of the scenes involving highly painted, sculpted figures had been amateurishly and cheesily staged, one such section having little boats being dragged across aluminium foil by nylon filaments. Thirdly, he did not know me and was stuttering on about commentary and effects here and there. But, Sam Smith came across in the sync-shot sequences as being a caring, humorous genius and I loved him. So I said, 'The only way I can do this film is for you to go away and leave me to it.' I made the whole soundtrack, taking the sync-shot sequences as set pieces to incorporate. While this was certainly not my normal approach to film and television work, it paid off here.

Since a piece of applied art is consumed/received/experienced as a whole, it should be made as a whole and it is possible for any specialist contributor to belong to this body of thinking right from the start. In the case of *Sam Smith – Genuine England*, it was a risky but simple combination of picture and me.

On an art/structure level, setting aside the story for a moment, to some extent I have always converted the picture into sound and the sound into picture in my head. This is a mild example of synaesthesia.[20] I do not think it is extraordinary, just to do with being immersed, belonging, enjoying the full experience. From a specialist maker's point of view, it also helps when the picture content is either not to your liking or not provocative or inspiring enough but you want to do a good job.

Taking the three minutes of little boats on aluminium foil, I focused on the patterns of colour and light and how they changed. To get started, I literally took some foil, gently crunched it up, made various copies of the recording, lowered the speeds (and of course pitch, being analogue tape), played some backwards, added reverb and I had a whole aluminium foil ocean for the boats. Sometimes, when you try this approach, the result is too busy, hard or characterful, but it leads you down another route, like taking an ocean and trying to bring it towards foil, or using paper instead as a starter, or scrapping all of this and doing it in the music. But I had my ocean and all I needed was to float some wafting misty chords on it which in turn supported a wandering melody representing the eye scanning the images, or maybe the hands originating them.

In contrast, for a BP series *History of the Motor Car* (British Petroleum, 1973–75)[21] one sequence was of a 1900's Renault, backlit by golden sun and shot through long wispy grass on a road in France. I composed a jaunty tune with a kind of engine-chug accompaniment on acoustic guitar set into a golden wash of chords. When I got to the 'dub' (final sound mixing session), the editor had the real engine sound running throughout. 'But it's in the music!' I shouted, believing the real sound to be superfluous and aware that it was masking some of the music elements anyway. I lost.

With today's technology it is perfectly possible for you as a film-maker to do all the sound and for me to edit all the picture. Maybe you are not going to come out with that special sound-structure that says so much more than a car-engine, but at least you might understand the need for homogeneity and organise early discussions with the sound creators. Then the composer (or sound artist) can send you a sound-sketch of an idea that may influence you to untold heights of dramatic dazzle – all part of the real dialogue of creativity. Since sound is at least half of the total experience, why is it not considered and incorporated at script stage? Get off that 'document' and into life.

The finished work may be assembled by many specialists, each one adding to the quality, but it is consumed as a whole experience, affecting the intellect and emotions as one. As a composer, or better, a fellow creative specialist, I always set out to belong to the team of any documentary I was working on. However, the old tradition of separate conception of script, picture, dialogue, voice-over, effects and music often leads to breakdown. Add to this the diverse interests of the production team and the commissioners, and my ideal is not often possible.

In the sound domain, the tradition of the picture editor laying effects and the composer composing 'music' is still far too common. On the one hand, many picture editors are so specialised in that field that they do not know about sound structure ('composition'). On the other, composers including myself sometimes use the picture as a vehicle for their suppressed virtuosity. What has happened is that the picture editor, being nearer to the director and therefore commanding a more powerful position in the hierarchy, has laid far more effects than necessary, anticipating unusable music, and some composers have now evolved to provide a lowest common denominator musical mush which will flow into any terrain of effects, under any amount of dialogue and voice-over, or will spoon into any forgotten hole.

None of these situations is satisfactory. Sound structure should be seen, understood and tackled as a whole – as the picture always has been. Whether that 'whole' is constructed by one person or a team is up to the skill of the management, usually represented by the director, but it could be a collective of every creative person on the project. This raises the question of: director, dictator or facilitator?

figure 12
creative sound manipulation

There will always be some conflict between skilled contributors. This conflict is often borne of mistrust, a mild type of fear of invasion, of one's passionate vision being interfered with. The creative team is not the size of a country; at its best it is a few caring souls who want to contribute their best specialisms to make a work which best articulates the truth as they see it.

One way is to use the new computer tools to bring specialists together for the overall strength of the work, to construct far more 'real' documentaries, or more bitingly contentious, opinionated and stirring.

In the documentary medium, you should consider and coordinate the necessary specialist channels of script, picture, dialogue, voice-over, effects and music so they best work together. I am including sync-environmental sound in 'effects' here, although in some other film forms, 'effects' are specifically 'spot effects', specially-positioned sound events 'post-synced', lined up to picture after shooting. Note that the last four are carried by sound, and that the tradition has been for the first three of these to be split off and handled by the editor. I urge you to change that tradition, either by coordinating all the sound lines, or by allowing a composer who shows an obvious command of sound homogeneity to coordinate them for you.

I find the traditional film-making stage 'storyboarding' to be incredibly thin and unsuitable for the medium. My proposal for a replacement and enhancement is a long and wide roll of paper – a rollboard? – even roleboard? Draw lines lengthways, maybe 5cms apart, then start at the left, draw a vertical line some way in, mark '0 seconds' at the top of it and start filling in material: time, story, pictures, scribbled notes, lighting instructions, commentary ideas, sound ideas – anything that comes to mind. You could put it on the floor and walk up and down it to see where you are. Later, you

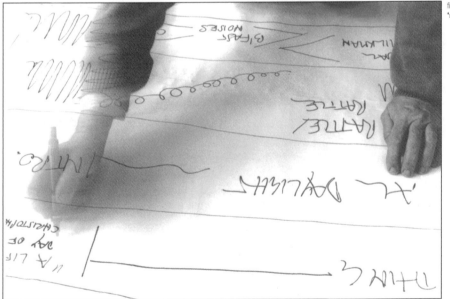

figure 13
'score'

could make a separate roll for the sound, or make the whole thing in a computer programme incorporating real stills and actual sound ideas.

If you are going to invite a composer into your cohesive team, they come in many forms. Little fat ones with handles on their backs which you turn and they spew out 'suitable' material – if you do not turn, you get nothing. Tall, thin, raving ones with bulging eyes and bird's nest hair, like the interminably complex material they spin out. Neatly dressed and briefcased ones who take accurate notes, and return with accurate notes. They all have something to offer. You have to work out whether you need it or not. Bearing in mind what I have said about specialists exhibiting 'fear of invasion', the best approach is the completely honest one. You can ask for a short demo CD/tape, which may be their standard issue, or one customised to your rough brief. Then you can say, 'This is only my second time', and talk openly about imagined problems and fears. But do it early, not two weeks before final delivery, otherwise you will need The Briefcase who will get the job done – mechanically. Several music colleges run specialist 'Media Composer' courses. These students need exercising.

The choice of real versus synthetic sounds is entirely yours. The meaning of synthesis is: making something by combining simpler, more fundamental, elements, sometimes with a bias towards the result being artificial or less genuine. I believe the whole process of film-making as an applied art is 'synthetic'. In the end, the object is to engage the viewer and somehow transport them into the world depicted. Sleight of hand is inevitable, even if it's only the hand that decides the beginning and end points of a timeline. The reasons for choosing one documentary style and then one sound style or sound ingredient in favour of another are as complex as the diverse and sometimes conflicting interests bearing upon the particular work. Also, too much thinking and worrying about fashion, style and commercial manoeuvrings prevents one from real expression.

Whether you're constructing a one-hour doc, a one-minute trailer, or any part of these, the hardest but most rewarding thing of all is to believe in what you're doing and not to let unnecessary complexities distract you ('keep it simple'). If you're anything like me, you'll have to go round most of the houses to get on the road. Rounding this chapter off as I began, surviving in and enjoying water is a matter of relaxed confidence with just the right amount of energy directed to propulsion. The underwater bit is that magical interweaving of lines to make meaning and art for stimulation and enjoyment.

NOTES

1 Hz = Hertz, after the German physicist H. R. Hertz whose name was given to the measurement in cycles per second of acoustic and electromagnetic waves in honour of his pioneering radio work. Therefore, 1Hz = 1 cycle/sec.

2 KHz = KiloHertz = one thousand Hertz.

3 See books on the physics of sound in Further Reading, below.

4 Hear Bobby McFerrin – see Further Listening, below.

5 Hear Hariprasad Chaurasia – see Further Listening, below.

6 See books on recording and equipment in Further Reading, below.

7 See also Level Control, under 'Processing'.

8 Also called 'lavalier'.

9 Sometimes sold as an acoustic guitar or piano transducer.

10 Try them on the pipes in a hotel basement!

11 'The Painter and the Pest' (Bandung Productions for Channel 4 TV, tx 2/5/1985). The painter was Harold Shapinsky.

12 'Splashpast', BBC Radio 4, tx 06/08/1993.

13 Such as Uher, Nagra, Stellavox.

14 'Automatic Gain Control' or 'Automatic Level Control'.

15 2x speed = 2x frequency = one octave up.

16 Reverberation: the sum of many different length repeat echoes.

17 A very useful booklet, Media Licensing, and other informative sheets are available from the Mechanical Copyright Protection Society (MCPS). Also, for contacting individual record companies and artists, see *Showcase – International Music Book*. Showcase Publications Ltd.

18 Two main ones in the UK are the Performing Right Society (PRS) and the Mechanical Copyright Protection Society (MCPS).

19 *Sam Smith – Genuine England* (Arts Council Films, 1976, dir. Dudley Shaw-Ashton)

20 Synaesthesia: the involuntary conversion of one sense to another.

21 *History of the Motor Car*, film series by British Petroleum: Part 1, 'The Dawn of Motoring' (1973); Part 2, 'The Veterans' (1973); Part 3, 'The Vintage Years' (1974). (Parts 4–6 not by Ron Geesin.)

FURTHER READING

Business and trade contacts:

Showcase: International Music Book (also available on CD ROM). London: Showcase Publications.

Miller, Lisa Anne (1998) *Film and Television Composer's Resource Guide: The Complete Guide to Organizing and Building Your Business*. Milwaukee: Hal Leonard.

Copyright:

Fishman, Stephen & Patti Gima (eds) (2000) *The Public Domain: How to Find and Use Copyright-Free Writings, Music, Art and More*. Nolo.com: USA.

Mechanical Copyright Protection Society, MCPS Guide to Media Licensing. London: MCPS.

Ears:

Pickles, James O. (1988) *An Introduction to the Physiology of Hearing*. London: Academic Press.

Philosophy of sound:

Berendt, Joachim-Ernst (1988a) *The Third Ear*. Dorset: Element Books.

____ (1988b) *Nada Brahma: The World Is Sound – Music and the Landscape of Consciousness*. London and The Hague: East-West Publications.

Cage, John (1968) *Silence*. London: Calder and Boyars.

Lanza, Joseph (1994) *Elevator Music*. New York: St. Martin's Press.

Shafer, R. Murray (1977) *The Tuning of the World*. New York: Knopf.

____ (1986) *The Thinking Ear*. Toronto: Arcana Editions.

Toop, David (1995) *Ocean of Sound*. London: Serpent's Tail.

Physics of sound:

Meyer, Erwin & Ernst-Georg Neumann (1972) *Physical and Applied Acoustics*. New York and London: Academic Press.

Richardson, E. G. (1953) *Technical Aspects of Sound, Vol. 1*. London and New York: Elsevier.

Psychology of sound:

Moore, Brian C. J. (1977) *An Introduction to the Psychology of Hearing*. London: Macmillan Press.

Recording and Equipment:

Amyes, Tim (1993) *Audio Post-production in Video and Film*. London and New York Focal Press.

Eargle, John (1976) *Sound Recording*. New York: Van Nostrand Reinhold.

White, Paul (1999) *The 'Sound on Sound' Book of Creative Recording*. London: Sanctuary.

FURTHER LISTENING

John Cage (twentieth-century composer): anything.

Hariprasad Chaurasia (master of the Indian bamboo flute):'Rag Bhimpalasi', Nimbus NI

5298 (CD); and any other Nimbus CDs.

Bobby McFerrin (voice and body): 'The Best of Bobby McFerrin', Blue Note CDP8533292; 'Voice', Wea/Elektra 7559603662.

Edgard Varèse (unique twentieth-century sound-texture composer) 'The Complete Works', Royal Concertgebouw Orch./ASKO Ensemble, Decca 460208-2.

USEFUL WEBSITES

www.focalpress.com – Focal Press

www.mcps.co.uk Mechanical – Copyright Protection Society

www.bl.uk/collections/sound-archive – National Sound Archive

www.nolo.com – Nolo.com

www.prs.co.uk – Performing Right Society

www.showcase-music.com – Showcase International

07 **digital technology and programme-making** colin denahy

Thirty years ago it took two strong men to lift what was effectively half a black and white broadcast camera. On the front of this unit, the camera head as it was called, were the three prime lenses (wide, medium, and long – no zoom lenses then!) and inside a small amount of electronics – small in function but very large in size by today's standards and very hungry for power. The camera head contained only part of the electronics needed for a working camera. The rest of the electronics were located in the Camera Control Unit (CCU). The connection between these two units was by thick, heavy, expensive multi-way cables, which often had to be moved by a person other than the camera operator: cable bashing as it was colloquially known.

Operating a camera was very labour intensive, using three or four people at a time per camera. It was a challenge, certainly, and looking back at the results, they were poor for all that effort.

Knowing how things were helps you understand how things came to be and why they are the way they are today: in the past, before digital equipment, we had analogue* equipment.

ANALOGUE SIGNALS AND SCANNING

Analogue systems record and transmit audio-visual data as a continuous signal, within a specified bandwidth. Analogue signals produce images by making white the brightest part of the signal equal to, or 'matched up' with 1 volt (the international standard for video and audio), and the black parts equal to 0.3 volt. The whole image is represented, therefore, by 0.7 volt. From 0 to 0.3 volt is allocated to signals which are used to synchronise the line and frame aspects of the images. To put this into context, the batteries which you put into a torch are 1.5 volts.

The image on a monitor or television is scanned from left to right: starting at the top left-hand corner it moves to the right-hand corner, then it moves down a little bit, approximately one sixth-hundredth of the image height, back over to the left and then the process starts all over again. It does this 625 times in one twenty-fifth of a second to produce a complete image – 25 complete pictures in a second. The system I have just described is the one used in Britain. The numbers may be slightly different in other parts of the world but the principles are the same. In the US, for instance, there are 525 lines and 30 complete pictures a second. This means that it has fewer lines per frame but more frames per second than the UK standard. In practice this means that you need a special system to view other standards on or to have them converted to suit your equipment. Conversion either way is a must if you want to use material of different standards in an edited item. While we are talking lines, frames and such, there is another term which you may have heard – interlacing. Even if the term is new to you it will be useful to understand its meaning, because you will come across it sooner or later.

Images are scanned from top to bottom in sequential horizontal lines. If you were to scan the image from the top to the bottom in numerical order – 1 2 3 4 5 etc, by the time you were just over halfway down the picture, the first line would have started to fade and by the time you got to the bottom it would have almost faded away – this

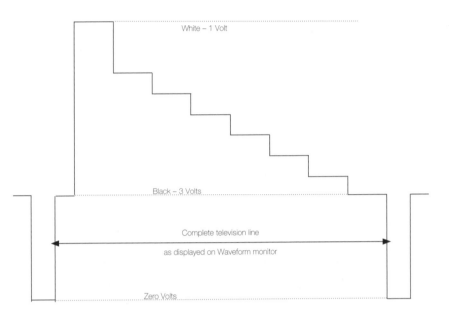

White – 1 Volt

Black – 3 Volts

Complete television line

as displayed on Waveform monitor

Zero Volts

figure 14
analogue system: typical video waveform – for clarity, only luminance (brightness) is shown

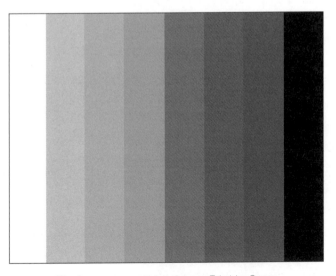

Waveform appears as picture above on Television Screen

would cause the picture to suffer severe flicker. The ingenious way round this is to scan the odd lines first and then go back and scan all the even. This means that you have one half of a picture (odd lines first) in the first fiftieth of a second and the other half (even lines) in the next fiftieth of a second: combine these two halves and you have one complete picture every twenty-fifth of a second, 25 pictures every second. In America it would be 60 half pictures and 30 complete ones. The numbers may vary across the world but the principles remain true. This is the what and why explanation of interlacing.

DIGITAL IMAGING

What is the difference between analogue and digital imaging? The easiest way to conceive of digital imaging is to think in terms of painting by numbers. In painting by numbers, the quality of the image is dependent on the size of the blocks of colour which make it up and the range of colours used to fill them. The digital system works by imaging the picture line by line etc, as per analogue images. To digitise the signal the system then chops the line up into little 'paint by numbers' pieces (the sampling rate) and each piece is assigned a numerical position coded in binary. It therefore stands to reason the more samples you take the finer the picture detail you can resolve. Having looked at the sampling rate the next thing to consider is how to describe the signal at the sampling points – this is known as the bit size. You need a large number of steps from black to white, and many colours, to make the details at each sampling point look realistic. The bit size is the number which represents the number of steps and detail assigned to the video signal at the sampling point and this is again recorded as a binary number.

The problem with analogue imaging is that it relies on signals being part on and part off to a very precise amount for most of the time and in such imaging consistency in this matching up process is difficult. In digital imaging, on the other hand, you represent the position and the signal value with a binary number. The binary system, having only two states – 0 and 1 (On/Off) – needs only switches. This makes the system more robust in representing signals and it does not suffer degradation in the same way that analogue does.

So if digital is so much better, why did we opt for analogue? The answer is available technology. Forty years ago transistors were not common and valves would have had to be used in their place. However, it was simply not a viable option to build the equivalent of a modern computer using valves.

For example, if the average Mac or PC desktop computer with 64 megabytes of ram in it uses approximately 600 million transistors, you would need 300 million valves, and each valve consumes 2 watts of energy just to heat it up and make it work, so 2 x 300 million = 600 million watts: this is enough power to run a housing estate.

Digital image recording

The development of 'chip' technology (millions of transistors in one small chip) has revolutionised the size and type of equipment available. An example is the modern digital camera; the single-chip camera produces great results, but the three-chip has the edge on quality.

The modern three-chip high-end domestic Digital Video Miniature (DVM) type camera shoots in standard 4:3 ratio and if you want widescreen it will also produce 16:9 ratio. The image and sound recorded are digital and as such are almost 'transparent', unlike the analogue counterpart.

The performance of the three-chip camera is excellent. In the past, video cameras needed quite a lot of light to produce good pictures, but with the three-chip digital camera good images are recorded at reasonable light levels. As an added bonus a lot of modern cameras are sensitive to infrared – a real plus for wildlife documentary.

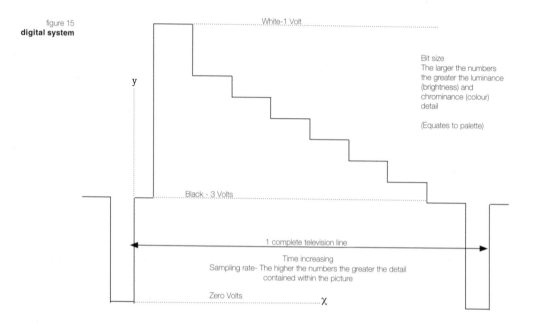

figure 15
digital system

White-1 Volt

Bit size
The larger the numbers
the greater the luminance
(brightness) and
chrominance (colour)
detail

(Equates to palette)

y

Black - 3 Volts

1 complete television line

Time increasing
Sampling rate- The higher the numbers the greater the detail
contained within the picture

Zero Volts

χ

The problem of battery life has been solved along with the digital camera. Once upon a time battery performance did not normally exceed one hour. Nowadays five to six hours is not unknown and this is a real bonus when you are out and about and do not want to be laden down with batteries. Digital cameras also have the advantage of having coloured viewfinders, so colour balance is much easier to get right than in the past when you only had a black and white viewfinder.

Finally, new generation digital cameras have shutter or iris-priority systems which offer similar control to an SLR analogue camera. Hence photographic/stylistic effects such as varying depth of field are achievable. The new small and light digital camera imposes less restrictions on the maker, and hence more opportunities are afforded you.

Computers and vision

Today, it is truly astounding what can be done with a modestly priced computer, a video capture card and a user-friendly piece of software. Let us consider recording and playback first. If you use a good compression system, and a compression ratio of about 10 to 1, even with a composite analogue input you can record and playback video from an SVHS source which will be almost indistinguishable from the original (and certainly better than an SVHS to SVHS copy). If you want even better quality use the SVHS lead (separate luminance and chrominance), but be careful plugging it in as the pins of the plug are quite fragile. If you use a card with a digital-in and digital-source system, then recordings really are like the original. You lose virtually nothing.

The higher the quality you demand then the more hard-drive* space you need. At 10 to 1 compression, you need approximately 1 gigabyte for every 10 minutes of recorded video. With the domestic Digital Video Miniature (DVM) system, which is around 5 to 1 compression, you get approximately 5 minutes of recording time for your 1 gigabyte of space. What all this means is that you do need large hard drives, but they are getting cheaper, and technology really is making it easier to produce better programs more easily and cost-effectively. *Adobe Premier* is a good middle-of-the-road, affordable video edit package although there are plenty more to choose from, some dearer or cheaper and with more or less facilities. What can you do with this program? The basic needs are cuts and mixes, which it can do, of course. Cuts are the basic industry tool and are extensively used in editing. Mixes (or dissolves) are not used as often in professional work as in amateur work.

Captions can also be achieved with *Adobe Premier*, which can be 'keyed' over a background. There are two sorts of keys – one is luminance, where you replace a chosen level of brightness in one picture with the elements from another. This can mean that if you have white captions on a black background you either replace the black with something else or you can replace the white. The next method of keying is called chroma-key or colour-separation overlay, and this works on the same principle as luminance except that instead of replacing a brightness level, you use a colour: this is normally blue which gives rise to its other name, 'Blue Screen'.

A key which you find in computers is the alpha key. This is a key analogous to the external key in conventional vision mixing circles, and is a third signal which may or may not be related to either of the other two signals. Its use is to 'cut holes' which can be filled with whatever you wish. You can produce, for instance, a key signal which does not change level quickly but does it gradually. If you choose an appropriate soft-edged transition then the gradual change of the key will produce a mix of the two signals. This is useful for seamlessly blending images together. There are dozens of other transitions

figure 16a:
making captions

Picture

Text

Combination of both
picture and text

figure 16b:
**composite digital
images, transitions**

Picture A

Separate Key
Ext Key
Alpha channel etc.

Picture B

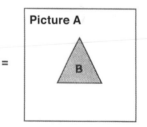

Composite of A+B
using Key channel

=

possible – for example page turns, horizontal and vertical wipes, diamond wipes and circular wipes. A word of advice here: go easy on the mixes and effects.

What else can *Premier* do? It can zoom in, zoom out, reverse footage so that it plays backwards, speed footage up, slow it down, adjust brightness, contrast, alter colour balance and so on. It can handle up to 99 video tracks and 99 audio tracks, depending of course on the speed of your computer.

One thing you must know is that it cannot make a silk purse out of a sow's ear. If your content is rubbish you can package it nicely but your programme will still be empty. Also, if your recording quality is poor, manipulation and the use of filters and so on will only make it look or sound different, which is not necessarily better.

DIGITAL AUDIO RECORDING

The system used to record audio is essentially the same as that used in video, using the binary system, where numbers are used to represent signals. What are the Digital Audio systems you are likely to come across? The first of these systems is Digital Audio Tape (DAT). The second is a Digital Compact Cassette system (DCC) which made a somewhat brief appearance in recent years. It offered excellent quality, but in my opinion was too late into the market, and before it could gain a foothold it was swept away by the mini disk. DAT is the system of choice in much of the professional market. Both DAT and DCC are tape-based systems but, unlike their analogue counterparts, they cannot be edited with a razor blade and sticky tape. This is because of the coding systems used. With DAT, you have the drawback that you need an extra system to edit on. The option which you most miss is 'Random Access' and this makes it time-consuming to use.

Random Access means that you can access any part of the audio without having to wind or rewind through other parts of the tape. Selecting your wanted track at the push of a button is so much easier than all that winding that you have to do on tape-based systems. You could buy a CD recorder and acquire your recordings on that, but if you get dust or dirt on the unburned CD it will scatter the laser light and you will have a faulty recording. This is not helpful if, say, the event that you are recording cannot be repeated.

What other options are there? There is the mini disk. I have often heard people say that they are worried about the system because it uses compression and so the quality cannot be as good as DAT. Well, yes: as a rule of thumb if you want to record the creaking of the fiddler's elbow use DAT. If, however, the sound of the violin is all you want to record the mini disk will be fine. I can, on a less frivolous note, assure you that the mini disk system is extensively used in radio and television throughout the world. The reasons for its universal adoption are its audio quality, its operational characteristics and its cost.

The advantages of the mini disk system are therefore excellent sound quality, random track access, track naming and editing in the machine. The editing allows you to join items together, cut sections out and re-order sections as required. In certain domestic machines you can even post fade the audio, rehearse edits and adjust in and out points until you are happy with the edit. It also has random play just like a CD and can also track repeat so it is handy if you want to make audio loops. The edits themselves are also silent and do not contribute clicks etc.

Having said all this about the mini disk, I hope that you can see that this is an enormous advance on what its nearest rival, the ¼" tape system, has to offer. These machines, great as they were in their time, are by modern standards' large and heavy, and require the use of razor blades, splicing tapes, cutting blocks, chinagraph pencils, good eyesight, and a steady hand to edit.

The mini disk is a great system but it cannot of course do everything, and this is where the computer enters to help and the fun really begins. What you need is a computer which has a way of getting your audio into it and enough disk space to record onto. Having got your computer and having played your audio into it and recorded it, we now come to the question of what can you do with the sound.

Computers and sound

I have just completed a 70-minute historical documentary project using a Pentium 133. Those of you who are computer literate will know that this is not a high-specification machine but is old and slow. The program I used is called *Soundforge*, which I find very user-friendly and intuitive, but there are other good programs out there and the choice is a question of what suits you.

It is a poor workman who always blames his tools: as makers of work, you do not have to have the latest technology or spend loads of money to do a decent job. What I achieved on a Pentium 133 and *Soundforge* was a composition made up of 2,000 edits, including soundscapes, standard type interviews and interviews in created sound spaces.

Using *Soundforge*, the process of cutting and pasting audio is made very simple because you get a visual representation of the waveform, which you can expand in both the X and Y directions (time and amplitude) to make editing easier and more precise. You can mix or insert atmosphere, sound effects or whatever, to make the edit more or less evident. Another function is the ability to vary the pitch of words (or parts of them) to help with the intonation. Getting the intonation right can often be a problem, especially in unscripted interviews, and the facility to be able to raise or lower levels of a small or large section of on-location, syncsound audio is, for instance, very useful.

You can also add, remove, modify and so on almost anything you wish and you do not have to start all over again if the change is in the middle, as was often the problem in a linear system. You can use equalizers, compressors, de-essers and de-poppers. You can make audio longer or shorter with or without changing the pitch. All you have to do is learn how the software works and practice with it. But please note again that if the recording is poor in the first place, the computer manipulation will only make it sound different, which is not to say better.

BROADCAST FORMATS AND NEW MEDIA

At one time it was quite apparent what were appropriate broadcast formats, for only certain equipment met specific engineering codes of practice. But now, with the advent of digital, a lot of what you see broadcast has come from high-end domestic as well as commercial equipment. Today the major and most obvious differences in the 'domestic versus professional' debate are evident in the quality of lighting, sound, content and construction.

Now 'broadcasting' exists as terrestrial, satellite, cable and the Net: all of these systems demand high-quality images except for one, the Net. If, in the case of webcasting, the recorded programme is full bandwidth (high resolution, lots of fine detail and movement), you have to send it a little piece at a time and assemble it at the other end if you wish to retain the detail and movement. This method gives good results but takes a very long time, too long in practice for most people to bother with. Compression can be used to reduce the time requirement. Data reduction systems mean you send less data: the less data the less time it takes to send it. One tool in the data reduction armoury is to look at the data, notice large areas which are the same and issue the command to display that until it changes: this is sometimes referred to as 'run until'. This saves you from having to describe every pixel and saves a lot of data.

When shooting for the Net, remember small pictures are viewed by the consumer, so nice big bold images will work well. The compression technique 'run until' dictates no fussy detailed backgrounds, and avoidance of pans, zooms, shaky hand-held shots, shots with lots of movement, or mixes. What works are shots which are low in detail and movement and are big and bold. If you are still not clear have a look on the Net and see what you think.

DIGITAL TECHNOLOGY AND IMPLICATIONS FOR PROGRAMMING ETHICS

As we have already discussed, in earlier decades equipment was difficult to use, heavy and expensive. This meant that most programmes were made in a formal way, in a relatively formal atmosphere. Programme-recording was far from spontaneous and so it was very difficult to get anything approaching a normal reaction from people on camera. Then social actors on camera were either well-known celebrities, 'victims', or 'experts', their views, lives and experiences not necessarily representative of the whole population. Today, however, there is wider participation by the public in documentaries.

Because equipment is now so light, easy to use and gives such very good results, programme-making is much more flexible and location work more straightforward than in the past. This, coupled with improved opportunities to manipulate material in post-production, means that the potential challenges facing programme-makers, of programme integrity and fair representation, are of paramount concern.

The current style of cheaply and quickly produced digital programmes rarely affords balanced debates and ethical rigour. With 24-hour television, unlimited channels, the Net etc., less time and money are available to the programme-maker per programme.

If today you now have a wider programming field and wider opportunities, you also have less time and less money to work with, and therefore you have to be more vigilant. In your quest for integrity and truth you must be aware that you can never represent absolute truth, only a personal and partial truth, as rigorously as you can.

08 **editing in non-fiction and documentary film** damian toal

The purpose of this chapter is to introduce the reader (user) to some of the technical, creative and aesthetic principles of editing both sound and image. By exploring the structure and mechanics of editing, its codes and conventions, we will explore the process of meaning constructed over space and time.[1]

At its simplest, editing is the transfer of pictures and sounds in analogue terms, from one tape to another and digitally from tape or disk to hard drive. Whether working on a linear tape-based system, or on a non-linear digital suite, one is able to copy original footage or camera tapes in whatever order, frequency and for whatever duration one chooses onto a new or master tape, replacing or repeating selective material as required.

This process represents the third and final stage of production development, following pre-production and production.[2]

Editing is above all an experimental and adaptive process, dependent upon an editor's understanding of how spectators read, interpret and process meaning through the moving image. The editor's role is fundamental in negotiating and realising a complex and often demanding dialogue between film-maker and audience. An editor must understand the specific technical and aesthetic principles of rendering and reproducing sound and image accurately, as well as undertaking the mixing of multiple sound tracks, supervising and producing graphics and so on. She/he mediates between the intentions of the script, the director and the expectations of the audience.

EDITING AS PART OF A PATTERNED AND FORMAL SYSTEM OF COMMUNICATION

In documentary we often expect an objective, unmediated and neutral record of life and events as they unfold before camera, with minimal interjection on the part of the director and editor. But as with fiction, the documentary film-maker must consider momentum, emotional peak and often drama, to ensure viewer interest and engagement. Therefore the notion of a simple or objective treatment, and notions of objective truth, become problematic.

The manipulation, selection and editing of material are interventions and distortions in themselves. Documentaries are affected and shaped by questions of ideology, bias and the point of view or ethos of the maker, broadcaster and audience. Emblematic and expositional images can also arouse empathy or disaffection in the audience. The editor has to tread a fine line between the aims of the production and the preconceptions and expectations of the viewer. These expectations are either met or denied by the editor: establishing tension, suspense and ultimately viewer participation, as questions are posed, relationships and the need for progression and resolution established. This is true of all forms of film and video production whether drama-based, promotional, experimental or documentary.[3]

Presenting a system of representation and visualisation is dependent upon a patterned, recognisable, and ultimately predictable use of sound and image in order to communicate a preferred reading.[4]

In non-fiction and documentary film the treatment, or stylistic approach taken, depends largely upon the makers and the subject or idea that is addressed by the programme. The programme can be organised within distinct categories, such as a predominantly historical format or the presentation of facts and related statistics in a seemingly objective manner.[5] An alternative treatment could present or discuss a given subject in an associational or abstract style, juxtaposing a series of interviews, vox pops* and voice-over with images in a more lyrical or non-specific way to suggest an idea, or evoke a strong emotional response from the viewer. A more rhetorical approach would be the presentation of an argument whereby a crisis or dilemma is established and identifying causes are discussed and ultimately a solution is posited. This is based on persuasion, with evidence presented to support this position or statement.

Although individual approaches such as these can be identified, more often than not the editor (in consultation with the director) will draw upon a combination of these structural types, often unifying these styles with narrative principles of interaction, 'individual stories', or testimonies, as well as emotive and surmounting drama.

The spectator engages with a film as with life, visually and phonetically by identifying key features, landmarks and objects in relation to themselves and the world about them, in order to establish a recognisable pattern and sense of place or order. These processes are exploited, manipulated and explored by the editor, by drawing upon the viewer's need for identification and assessment. The editor must establish a suitable vocabulary to describe and communicate intent through the association of specific voice-over and image with specific ideas and related themes.

Both sound and picture conform to subsystems of similarity and difference, with repetition of significant sounds and images establishing recognisable patterns and meaning through motif. For example, a long shot of a woman walking on a beach, juxtaposed with a voice-over or interview talking about divorce, could suggest a motif for associated loneliness or freedom, depending on the particular contextual sound or voice-over.

Dialogue, ambient sound, and non-diegetic sound all support and inform the narrative's progression, often providing subtext as well as context. This allows the editor to present parallel themes or issues that lie beneath the surface of the principal arguments, as well as comment directly on their significance or explicit meaning.[6]

In order to establish the significance of sound and image in relation to one another, whether literally or figuratively, the editor relies heavily on repetition, which is fundamental to our understanding of any film. We must be able to recall and recognise characters, and their relationship to the argument and each other, each time they reappear. Through this, the viewer is able to recall questions or conflicts established within characters and the film as a whole.

Through editing one must reconstruct, articulate, and present an often complex and difficult argument or debate around issues the viewer may or may not have any prior knowledge or appreciation of. On one level we are concerned with constructing a dialogue and presenting information in a clear and lucid way. On the other hand we also signal and communicate observations and conclusions which may challenge the viewer's preconceptions and any simple interpretation of questions raised.

With this in mind, it is the editor's job, by drawing on the viewers' previous experiences through media and life, to construct a series of images and sounds which present both the principal argument and related themes (what is made explicit and what is implied) in an accessible, challenging and appropriate way.

THE PRINCIPLES OF EDITING

Off-line and on-line editing

The off-line edit provides the editor with the first opportunity to construct or assemble the first cut or rough draft, outlining the production's shape and form, the order and duration of shots and so on. Relying on simple cuts only, the shots are blocked

figure 17
digital editing suite

in without dissolves or effects. This allows the editor to test the required tone or emphasis of a given structure and determine an appropriate treatment, as well as identify any shortcomings.

Ordinarily, with expensive formats like DV and BetaCam, the tapes are transferred to a cheaper format like VHS. This enables the editor to work in a less expensive edit suite until she/he is sure of all the cuts required. This process of transfer also protects the field tapes or originals from any possible tape damage as an off-line can take some time, and the tapes come under considerable stress. When working digitally, source tapes are digitised or copied onto the hard drive at a smaller compression ratio or size in order to free up storage space and enable the system to process a large amount of material.

Using the off-line edit as a template or reference, the editor will then reconstruct or auto-conform the off-line edit using the original tapes and conforming video and sound to the requirements of broadcast standards and quality. This is known as the on-line, and is the final edit with all mixes, dissolves and visual effects applied. It is normally at this stage that the final sound edit is completed as well as titles and credits applied. In a broadcast production, this cut takes place in a sophisticated and consequently expensive edit suite, and in order to spend as little time as possible in the suite, all the major decisions will have been made at the off-line stage.[7]

In order to edit effectively, you need to understand a little about how the video signal is recorded and then 'read' on video tape. There are a number of component parts on a video tape, the largest of which is the picture track, which occupies the centre of the tape. On the edge of the tape are two mono audio tracks (as well as the HI FI tracks: interlaced within the picture track) and finally a control track or timecode. The control track works in much the same way as the sprocket holes on film. Video decks and controllers use the control track or timecode to ensure that the tape is travelling at the correct speed (frame rate) in order for each editing deck to synchronise and ensure frame accurate editing and play back.

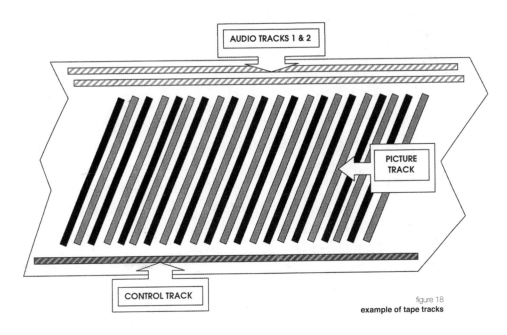

figure 18
example of tape tracks

Assemble editing

As with a domestic video machine, when you press record you create an assemble edit. That is, you copy all of the component parts of a signal from one tape to another (i.e. video signal, audio tracks and control track or timecode). This means that you can sometimes get 'jumps' between pictures where the control track or timecode is broken.

This is the simplest form of linear editing, enabling you to assemble a sequence of shots one after the other in whatever order is required. The disadvantages of this system are that you cannot edit the sound or picture separately, and you cannot go back and replace a shot without disrupting playback by re-recording and breaking the original control track.

Insert editing

When you insert edit, you lay the control track down first, in the form of a continuous signal. This is known as 'blacking' your master tape, onto which you are then able to edit both picture and or sound without disturbing or re-recording the timecode or control track. This means that there is a clean transition between shots and picture playback is consistent. This also ensures frame accuracy when determining where a shot will start and where it will end. Unlike assemble editing, insert editing enables the editor to edit sound and picture simultaneously as well as independently. So in order to edit effectively we need to ensure when working within a linear or tape based environment to select 'insert edit'.

Most editing suites will still allow you to select assemble mode in order for you to black your tape before selecting insert edit.

PLANNING FOR POST-PRODUCTION

The form, treatment or stylistic approach taken when producing documentary film depends largely upon the overall aims and objectives of the programme. We can identify two key approaches to the planning, research and development of a given programme.[8]

The planned approach

Based on the production and development of a script and treatment, a planned approach evolves through screenplay, storyboard and shooting script etc. This structured or systematic approach establishes the aims and objectives of a production, providing clear objectives and a means of focus and co-ordination for post-production. Conversely, the production can become bogged down in organisation, lacking spontaneity and appearing predictable or formulaic in its treatment of subject matter. Opportunities can be missed or ignored through logistical restraints and pressures of timetable and so forth. This system relies upon good continuity and careful pre-production.

As more experimental forms of documentary and non-fiction film have evolved, adaptive and new approaches to production have been identified. One is a loosely structured or empirical approach to documentary production.

The empirical approach

Based on a collection or sequence of shots related to a general theme or idea, an empirical approach to production is one based on observation and experimentation rather than on a system or specific script. Using a series of atmospheric and associative shots filmed in response to an initial Idea, a film-maker/editor will prepare a script/edit that fits and interprets the material at hand, whether interview-based, or using found footage or archive material. This approach often incorporates a single unifying system or rhetoric such as a voice-over to provide context and establish significance and confer meaning upon what we see. The voice-over can often be at odds with the material's original context or singular meaning. This approach is opportunistic and avoids rigid discipline allowing both crew and participants to contribute to the interpretation of text or script.

At best, an empirical approach allows us to produce a production which is dynamic, uninhibited and improvisational; which makes use of the unexpected and allows us to fully realise the potential and relevance of material gathered (which may not have survived a traditional translation from script to finished product).

At its worst, such an approach can be haphazard, producing a sequence of unrelated and confused images that can lack purpose and cohesion. Coherent editing becomes difficult and the development or exploration of themes and relationships between players becomes impossible. Good documentary practice, and subsequently editing, depends on developing a balance between a planned or scripted approach, and a more spontaneous empirical approach.[9]

Before we can analyse our material properly, we must first make an accurate record or log of the material at hand.

Logging and preparing to edit

Working from our rushes, we must first determine what material we can use and what – for any technical or aesthetic reasons – we are unable to use. It is important to allow our material to evolve from the strict requirements of our original text or script, and to be open to any opportunities or observations which we could not have planned for or were unforeseen.

table 2 **log sheet**

in	out	duration	take	comments	sound
00/03/00/12			1	INT. C/U OF TEACHER / CENTER FRAME	'PLEASE TURN TO
				TALKING TO CAMERA / HOLDING PEN.	PAGE NINE…
00/05/32/20				CAM. PULLS TO WIDE / TEACHER TAKES	
				OFF GLASSES / DOOR LEFT OF FRAME.	
	00/11/00/12	00/08/00		CHOOSES GIRL FRONT ROW TO READ	…CONTINUE JANE'
00/11/00/12			2	AS ABOVE BUT TEACHER WEARING	FLUFFS FIRST LINE
	00/19/32/06	00/08/32		GLASSES	
00/19/32/07			1	EXT. L/S OF PLAYGROUND / BOYS IN	CHILDREN OFF
				FOREGROUND PLAYING FOOTBALL	SCREEN SINGING
				SCHOOL IN BKGD. / TEACHER C FRAME.	RING A RING A ROSES
	00/21/12/22	00/02/44		CHILDREN RUNNING L TO R / OVERCAST	

Unlike the director, the editor does not ordinarily have a personal investment in the material and so can be far more objective when it comes to revealing any problems that are inherent, such as poor continuity or poor sound/picture quality. This objectivity allows the editor to develop strategies such as splitting sound and picture or the use of cutaways in order to resolve such problems.

It is important to differentiate clearly between one shot and another as well as between scenes. To begin logging, rewind the tape to beginning and if using control track (S VHS/VHS/U–MATIC), zero the counter on the edit controller at the beginning of the picture not at the beginning of the tape. Knowing the requirements of the editor, the cameraman would have allowed for pre-roll time (at least 10 sec.) and bars and tone (approximately 2 min.).

Control track and timecode numerals enable the editor to catalogue and locate accurately the frame at the beginning and end of each new shot, and log each new take or shot as they appear on tape followed by a brief description of events as they unfold. It is important to keep comments brief; describing the dimensions of shot, whether close up or long shot and so on, and the movement of subject or object in relation to the frame and internal space (foreground, mid-ground and background etc).

The log should comment upon aspects that relate to continuity such as staging, break in picture or sound or fluffed lines and so on. It should also comment on the relationship of subject/object to viewer: whether left of frame, or centre etc. The log should also highlight the movement of camera within the frame for any new takes of a previous shot.

The control track's numeric reference of hours, minutes, seconds, and frames (25f per sec.) is not fixed (unlike timecode), so it is important not to reset your counter when logging. Although labour intensive, logging is invaluable for not only determining the shots required, but also for familiarising yourself with the internal pace and feel of the work as a whole. On a more practical note, scrutinising the work in such detail enables you to identify potential solutions for any problems which may arise when sound or picture is missing, damaged or inappropriate in the overall sequence.

The next step, working from our log sheets, is to mark off against the script shots required and produce an edit decision list (EDL) from which we now work to produce our rough cut. All interviews should be transcribed and typed up.

POINTS TO CONSIDER WHEN ORGANISING AND ASSEMBLING MATERIAL

Non-fiction, just like fiction, is dependent on a degree of drama or tension in order to motivate and allow the viewer to participate in the events as they unfold. In order to make these connections, it is important to identify an axis of action whereby the following issues are addressed: how a scene or shot effects or informs what has gone before, what its significance is in the overall debate or argument, and whose point of view is represented and why? This is about establishing focus and emotional impact as well as encouraging an audience to empathise with, oppose, or question what is being presented.

In order for the viewer to negotiate and appreciate the relationship between these often multiple angles of tension it is important to establish a strategy of concealment and revelation: what does the viewer need to see at any given time and how do we introduce, seed and organise complex ideas or relationships? It is important to determine the relationship between viewer and action, whether it is observational (objective) or participational (subjective).[10] It is therefore important, within a given scene as well as with the programme as a whole, to establish thematic purpose and a means of identification for the viewer in light of the presentation of new and important information, plot development and emotional peaks. We do this by associating and representing ideas and related debates which lie beneath the surface of our text (subtext) or principal argument with emblematic and evocative choice of representation and the relationship and pattern of shots we choose.[11]

For example a long shot or medium wide shot establishes context and provides an overview of subject and related themes both literally and metaphorically. With a medium shot/two shot we begin to focus on both subject and object depicted in greater detail, and are able to begin to speculate and make connections between subject and objects within the frame. A close up isolates a subject or detail and specific aspects described either visually or phonetically.

Of course one is able to subvert these conventions when appropriate: for example, when we hear confrontational and disembodied dialogue which, for instance, may be at odds with a seemingly sedate long shot of a row of houses (the subtext of which hints at a misleading veneer of normality). But this process of association and revelation is crucial in establishing a rapport with the spectator.

PRODUCING A ROUGH CUT

Working from your EDL, script and transcripts, the first thing to consider is a programme's basic outline or structure. It is important to identify and lay down in large blocks the principal shots, scenes and sync sound in the order required, avoiding any fine editing, cutaways, or close ups etc. After reviewing this first cut, one is able to test the script or outline against what footage is available and what is missing, and ascertain any likely change in the logic or order of shots laid down.

This is the first opportunity to determine the programme's overall balance and tempo and to establish where appropriate punctuation (cutaways, voice-over, rostrum work and so on) is required. In critical terms, one is able to test how accessible and comprehensible a given flow of ideas or argument is likely to be to an audience, and how relevant your coverage. The editor has also to take into account the work's overall development, its dramatic and emotional impact as well as determine an appropriate programme length and pace.

After completing our initial edit, the flow or development of an argument is still likely to be disjointed and erratic. In order to communicate and develop our programme in an articulate and fluid manner, we need to make some implied and literal connections in time and space to unify both sound and image so that the spectator will better understand the material.[12] The editor is able, when assembling relevant material, to associate and establish visual and aural unity in several ways:

Compositional or graphic relationships between shots

This covers all aspects of composition, from patterns of similarity and difference of objects or subjects in the frame, to patterns of light and dark (tone) and colour. These graphic qualities can be edited to achieve continuity, balance and symmetry from one shot to another, or to establish a break or abrupt contrast in image and sound.

Graphically, shots that are selected should be suitably composed, either matching or reflecting the general dynamic/movement and visual structure of the preceding or following shot. Badly composed shots are not only difficult for the viewer to assimilate, but can be difficult to cut together regardless of content or their importance to narrative comprehension.

Discontinuous matches can also be appropriate. For example, when shooting and editing together two interviews or pieces to camera, it is appropriate to place/film one subject left of frame and the other right of frame. This establishes counterpoint and difference and can reinforce a theme of conflict or opposition as well as dramatic tension, while also avoiding what appears to be a jumpcut.

Spatial unity or difference

This same example or technique can unite subjects or interviewer and interviewee, often filmed at separate times or locations, with matching eyeline and overlapping audio, creating spatial unity. Again compositionally, the centre ground unites them and they appear to inhabit the same space and time. This enables the editor to construct a harmonious and unified space out of separate and component parts through the viewer's assumption of spatial co-existence.[13]

Temporal and rhythmic relations between shots

The editor controls the time or duration of action, how many times we experience it, and its order. The frequency and duration of a given shot or scene establishes accent, beat and tempo. The editor controls the amount of time the spectator has to grasp and reflect upon what is seen. This builds tension and suspense and – like music – gratification. Varying shot duration allows the editor to accentuate or decentuate a given moment, allowing the viewer to appreciate the significance and importance of a given scene.

The time a shot remains on screen will depend on several factors. Firstly, one must consider whether the action and information can only be shown in full, or whether its exposition or duration could disrupt the overall pace and/or distract from more central points. If this is the case, this information must be compressed or extended for dramatic purposes in its presentation. This can be achieved by the insertion of a cutaway or other forms of punctuation such as a fade, dissolve, or parallel action etc. In documentary, emphasis or importance of a participant can be achieved through the temporal manipulation of these techniques, as well as the overlapping of sound and/or image.

DEVELOPING THE FINE CUT

Following the rough cut, we can now begin to address specific and localised questions concerning the edit: questions of rhythm, pace, patternation and accessibility. This diagnostic questioning allows us to prioritise and assess why material is not working and whether we have to adapt our treatment or approach.

Below are key points to consider and questions to ask when outlining and evaluating your fine cut, in order to determine what the audience needs to see and hear in your documentary.

Audience: It is important to determine appropriate and accessible terms of reference, and identify issues of identification or appeal for relevant audiences.

• what is the target audience?

• how familiar is your audience with the subject matter?

• is the work for broadcast, or a more specialist market?

What is the purpose of the film?: The aims and objectives of your film will directly affect questions of representation, development and the emphasis of your argument as well as its tone.

• does the film examine a process, technique or institution (e.g. expositional or investigative)?

• is the documentary instructional (e.g. a training film)?

• does the film need to present and analyse information or data (e.g. economics, scientific, statistics etc)?

• is the film a study of current affairs or the interview of a person/personalities?

Structure: It is essential that the composition of your film be appropriate:

• is the film long enough to effectively explore a broad range of topics or arguments?

• does the film need to recap or reaffirm any previous information or rhetoric?

• is there adequate coverage? If not, do you need to re-shoot or can you use alternative means such as archive material or rostrum work?

• if film length is short, is it appropriate to make an impact at the beginning?

• do you need to establish a historical precept or context?

• if the subjects or themes are abstract or inaccessible, how will you illustrate them?

Assimilation of information: Keep your thesis or argument simple – do not be overly complex or exclusive in your terms of reference and use of language.

• is the viewer overloaded with too much information?

• do the accompanying graphics or metaphorical images help to clarify or illustrate more complex or abstract ideas?

• is your coverage clear and concise and to the point? It is easier to do justice to a few related and central themes than to cover too many points and lose your audience.

• does the film allow suitable screen time and punctuation, such as a fade to black or slow dissolve, to allow the viewer to assimilate or take on board any complex information or emotionally powerful emphasis or transition? If there is text on screen, is there enough time for the viewer to read and take on board its meaning and significance?

• does any accompanying voice-over reinforce textual information as well as provide emotional emphasis and context?

Developing a flow of ideas: Be sure of your aims and objectives when developing your argument, allowing adequate screen time to cover points effectively. Questions to ask yourself are:

• what is it essentially you want to say or explore about your subject?

• are there any instances of contradictory or divisive audio and visuals, that run counter to what is being described or explored (for example, the images of a serious or sombre subject with upbeat or inappropriate soundtrack or testimony)?

• does one subject or sequence lead naturally into the next?

• does the film punctuate topics with the use of a transitional motif or emblem such as a recurrent image or sound which relates or evokes an underlying feeling or subtext, (for example, the use of cutaways to an airport and scenes of imposing immigration officers, inter-cut between testimonies of political refugees, would not only break up or punctuate individual stories but also evoke a strong sense of fear and stigma on behalf of someone seeking asylum, as well the sub-text of political and social intolerance, thus providing a means of identification or empathy for the viewer).

• does the subject or thesis require an introduction or can we personalise the issues through individual testimony?

• does the work require a resolution or summary of main points and conclusions reached?

• is the pace of the programme varied according to the importance and significance of issues presented? A fast pace will inhibit the conveyance and reading of important information, but can be useful for conveying a sense of excitement, confusion or dynamism. If the pace becomes too slow, the viewer becomes bored and easily distracted.

SUMMARY OF GUIDELINES FOR EDITING DOCUMENTARIES

1. There should always be an appropriate reason or motivation for an edit or cut from one shot to another. Visually this can be determined by an action or movement within the frame, cutting from one action or counteraction to another, long shot to close up etc: aurally this can be from one interview to a counter-interview. More subtly, a change of audio or music can precipitate or foreshadow some incoming sequence, setting a new tone or parallel action that can be cut to.

2. Each new shot should aim to provide new information or provide a different perspective for the viewer. The aural or visual information could be about an individual element or participant within the production, either providing some new insight or background information within a given scene, or it could simply represent the next stage of the narrative. (Note: when cutting between two shots of different subjects, try to find some decisive moment which will carry the eye through to the next shot, following a movement or glance, for example, from left to right of frame.)

3. Sound is a tremendously important aspect of the editing process. It can provide information, emotional peaks or context that for practical or emotive constrictions could

not be represented visually. However, above all, be visual: do not use superfluous or irrelevant accompanying sound or voice-over.

4. Too much visual information or rapid editing can distract from important dialogue or voice-over.

5. Punctuate talking heads with relevant or revealing cutaways.

6. Remember not to talk down to your audience, and be creative visually – avoid obvious or literal treatments.

7. Remember the repetition of appropriate visual motif can reinforce or remind the viewer of central points or issues.

8. Always allow a bold camera movement to finish before cutting to the next shot.

9. Avoid placing too many moving shots (panning/zooming) together. Contrast a static shot with a moving one.

10. Always try to match eyeline to ensure spatial continuity.

These are some aspects of good practice which will allow you to be consistent and thoughtful when developing what is in effect an extremely complex and demanding skill. Good editing comes essentially from observation: understanding both the audience and the requirements of brief. A good editor is essentially pro-active, adapting to logistical and technical restraints or problems and using his or her critical facilities and problem solving skills.

Not all of these are learned skills.

NOTES

1 For further reading see N. Carroll (2000) 'The Specificity of Media', in R. Stam & T. Miller (eds) *Film and Theory: An Anthology*. Oxford: Blackwell, 39–54.

2 Each stage is interdependent, and requires a clear understanding of the linear nature of development and the requirements of each stage of production.

3 For further insight into the comparative qualities with fiction, see M. Renov (ed.) (1993) *Theorising Documentary*. London: Routledge, 5–7.

4 As determined by the maker's point of view. The experiences and cultural and social identities of individual spectators bring an added dimension which forces the film-maker to accommodate alternative readings and address issues of communality and shared lived experience.

5 For a working definition of structural types or modes of address within documentary, see B. Nichols (1985) 'The Voice of Documentary', in *Movies and Methods, Vol. 2*. Berkeley: University of California Press, 258–73. This should not be taken as a definitive outline, as modes of address change over time and theoretical positions conflict.

6 This process works subconsciously, supporting and substantiating the maker's position and point of view.

7 This can also be achieved by a 'Paper Edit', drawing upon transcripts, log sheets and script, in order to produce an Edit Decision List (EDL) or 'paper' first cut.

8 As defined by G. Millerson (1992) *Video Production Handbook*. London: Focal Press, 160.

9 As with fiction, we must consider plausibility and issues of continuity – if not spatially, then psychologically – as well as providing adequate coverage.

10 See K. Silverman (1983) *The Subject of Semiotics*. Oxford: Oxford University Press, 205.

11 The use of rhetorical or organisational strategies does not preclude an 'inner truth' but does challenge the notion of 'objective truth'.

12 Like mainstream continuity editing in fiction, the development of plot, action and the representation of characters or participants within documentary can often be subordinate to a sense of storyline or plot development. This is to ensure that the viewer is not distracted from the persuasive influence of the programme's inner world.

13 See Lev Kuleshov's theory of 'creative geography' in J. Monaco (1981) *How to Read a Film*. Oxford: Oxford University Press, 308–9.

BIBLIOGRAPHY

Barrow, E. (1993) *Documentary: A History of the Non Fiction Film.* Oxford: Oxford University Press.

Bordwell, D. & K. Thompson (1993) *Film Art: An Introduction.* London: Knopf.

Bruzzi, S. (2000) *New Documentary: A Critical Introduction.* London: Routledge.

Carroll, N. (1996) *Theorising the Moving Image.* Cambridge: Cambridge University Press.

Hayward, S. (2000) *Cinema Studies: The Key Concepts.* 2nd edn. London: Routledge.

Hodges, P. (1989) *Video Measurement: An Introduction.* London: Focal Press.

Lusted, D. (1991) *The Media Studies Book.* London: Routledge.

Millerson, G. (1992) *Video Production Handbook.* 2nd edn. London: Focal Press.

Monaco, J. (1981) *How to Read a Film.* Oxford and London: Oxford University Press.

Nelmes, J. (ed.) (1996) *An Introduction to Film Studies.* London: Routledge.

Nichols, B. (1985) 'The Voice of Documentary', in *Movies and Methods, Vol. 2.* Berkeley: University of California Press, 258–73.

Rabinger, M. (1989) *Directing: Film Techniques and Aesthetics.* London: Focal Press.

Reisz, K. & G. Millar (1968) *The Techniques of Film Editing.* London: Focal Press.

Renov, M. (ed.) (1996) *Theorizing Documentary.* London: Routledge.

Silverman, K. (1983) *The Subject of Semiotics.* Oxford: Oxford University Press.

Stam, R. & T. Miller (2000) *Film and Theory: An Anthology.* Oxford: Blackwell.

USEFUL WEBSITES

www.videonics.com/articles/

www.puremotion.com/glossary/index.htm

www.quantel.com/editingbook/editingterms.htm

www.internetcampus.com/tvpo56.htm

www.iimages.com/glossary.html

Industry contacts

www.digitalvideoediting.com/Htm/DVEditHomeSet1.htm

www.uky.edu/MCFACTSCenter/tutorials/premiere/editPREMIERE.html.

www.ironduke.CS.gsu.edu/~gsowen/present/videotalk/capturing_video.htm

www.puremotion.com/videoediting/articles/gettingstartedindesktopvideo/index.htm

www.learneringcenter.clayton.edu/fidl/video/adobepreiere.htm

www.film-makercom/editing

coda **streaming media and documentary** william garrison and searle kochberg

In Chapter 7, Colin Denahy referred to documentary on the web. Streaming media is a collection of technologies that allow the delivery of moving images across the Internet, whereby video is highly compressed and delivered on demand to each viewer. It works something like this: a viewer in Bulgaria finds an interesting website on the Internet and clicks a video link. Across the globe in Australia a video server receives the request. The server polls the user to estimate the ability of the Internet to carry video to this particular user. Once the server has tested the connection, it begins sending packets of video data at a suitable rate or bandwidth. These packets make their way across the globe, possibly by different routes, arriving in a different order than they were sent. The viewer's computer collects the packets, reorders them, corrects for any lost packets, decompresses the video and displays it on the screen. The result is that the user is able to view the video stream of their choice on demand.

In principle, streaming media is very straightforward. For the viewer, it is a simple, seamless and reliable process, no more difficult than clicking on a standard link. In practice, it does require a lot of technology that has to be provided and managed. But it is not unreasonable for computer-savvy individuals to create and deliver their own streams in the same way as anyone can publish web pages.

Today's technologies: implications for makers – opportunities and challenges

Streaming media is a new conceptual process whose form and aesthetics have yet to be decided. Audiences for it are huge and transcend national and geographic boundaries. However, most of these viewers are unable to receive more than a trickle of data at present, and therefore the resulting image is of poor quality. The flexibility and pervasiveness of the Internet, coupled with the limited bandwidth of most connections, places new demands on film-makers.

In this nascent period of streaming media, there has been a lot of emphasis placed on the creation of images that work well at low bandwidths. This means that the film-maker must be aware of how streaming media affects the quality of images and should consider his/her aesthetic style so that it makes good use of the medium.

The compression algorithms used to create video streams do have an aesthetic impact, and when producing for streaming media the following recommendations are worth considering:

- ensure images are well-exposed and well-lit.
- create simple images with sharp lines and high contrast.
- use a tripod.
- avoid pans, zooms and other forms of camera movement.
- avoid dissolves or other effects.
- avoid unnecessary cuts or fast-paced editing.
- pay special attention to sound recording and mixing.

But do not let the above recommendations restrict you unduly: for instance, if you want to create a sense of grandeur of a forest, then dolly, pan, tilt, zoom, or dangle from a helicopter! Film-makers who craft work only for a small, fuzzy screen, ultimately limit the distribution potential of that work. If streaming media technologies are improving at a phenomenal rate, work should be designed for exploitation across a multitude of e-media anyway.

The future: documentary and streaming media

The history of documentary film-making is marked by a struggle for funding and distribution. Reality TV apart, audience demand for documentaries has been marginal compared with other forms of entertainment, and hence broadcast networks and distributors have often been reluctant to handle them in great numbers. Streaming media has the potential to change this, for it is revolutionising the distribution of moving images in the same way that the Internet has revolutionised publishing.

The real power of streaming media lies not in a new delivery of existing genres, but in the development of an entirely new product combining the interactive power of the Internet with the rich moving images of film-making. Future works, documentary or otherwise, will be composed of much more than moving images. Future works will be highly interactive, engaging the viewer in ways that are only now becoming possible. This new medium is often referred to as 'Rich Media' because it integrates everything that is the Internet with the power and immediacy of television. This union – between the interactivity of the Internet and the richness of moving image – offers immense new opportunities for expression and creativity.

Imagine documentaries that contain real-time information from web-cams, news feeds or other sources. Imagine in-depth, long-form interviews in addition to the brief choices made by the director. Imagine cross-linking your works with the works of other documentary film-makers so that viewers can instantly compare different treatments of the same topic. Imagine parallel storylines that are no longer an editor's cliché, but rather a new way of engaging with the content. Documentaries such as *The Thin Blue Line* could be crafted in such a way as to allow the viewer the ability to construct his/

her own engagement with each of the testimonies of the witnesses on his/her own terms.

The technologies necessary to create these new forms of documentary media exist and are accessible. What is lacking is *content*. If the traditional art of film-making is well understood by the makers and their audiences, this new medium is breaking all the rules and opening new horizons for an imaginative wave of new creation.

Students in multidisciplinary groups are in an ideal environment to collaborate on non-fiction streaming media projects. A streaming media project designed by a team of web designers, documentary video makers, computer animators and graphic designers could illuminate new possibilities in non-fiction/documentary product.

The technology works well and continues to improve: what is needed is content. So go forth and create new and imaginative non-fiction interactive media.

USEFUL WEBSITES

For hosts and distributors of short films on the web see:

www.atomfilms.com

www.ifilm.com

For funding, mentoring and tools for college students to create new video content for the Internet see:

www.nibblebox.com

For viewing other makers' work and meeting them face to face, you will need to visit film festivals such as:

The Sheffield International Documentary Festival: www.sidf.co.uk

International Documentary Film Festival Amsterdam: www.dds.nl/ ~damocles/idfa

Hot Springs Documentary Film Festival: www.hotspringsar.com/hsdff/

glossary

Analogue: An adjective applied to any system or device that records and transmits audio-visual data as a continuous signal, within a specified bandwidth, which is subject to degradation and change over space and time.

Antirealism: A strategy used by many makers of film to attack what they see as the illusionism of Realism. Here the formal and structural elements of a production are brought to the fore self-consciously in an attempt to activate and provoke the spectator.

Associative Editing: An approach to editing which is very common in documentary, where shots are edited together to establish their metaphorical or symbolic relationships. Hence a structure is created which brings out the theme of a work, as opposed to developing a plot based upon cause/effect relations.

Auteur: A term meaning 'author' and coined by the magazine, Cahiers du Cinéma, in the 1950s to describe a director whose authorial style is distinguished by a significant theme and/or visual style. The notion of a director as an artist can, at times, be applied too rigidly, so that all films of one maker are interpreted as important, and worth seeing, whilst films of 'non-artists' can languish in obscurity.

Axis of action: An imaginary line or axis between players or performers along which drama and focus are exchanged.

Bars and tone: A test signal to calibrate the luminance, chrominance and sound levels of a video signal, to ensure continuity and broadcast standards are maintained.

Broadcast standard: This refers to the standardised system of calibrating, recording and transmitting video, i.e. PAL, SECAM, NTSC, etc. Each element of the signal, chrominance, luminance etc is measured and reproduced according to prescribed practice. For example, with the PAL system, black is determined as 0.3 volts, while white is 1.0 volt.

Classic Realism: The term refers to a format based on seamless causal logic. Through editing and voice-over, the spectator is guided through events, and any 'loose ends' tend to be resolved by the end of the documentary.

Codes and conventions: A set of rules, cues or signals employed visually and technically, which are specific to a genre. These provide the spectator with guidelines for interpreting and participating in a film. For example, within documentary, a lack of formal lighting, break in continuity, voice over and interview can signal authenticity and objective observation.

Colour temperature: This is the colour quality of a light source measured in degrees Kelvin. Daylight and studio lights have different colour temperatures, and to even out differences in colour quality, you have to adjust the camera's white balance or use different gel filters.

Compression ratio: The proportional relationship between original audio-visual data and the size of a compressed file, e.g. 10:1, 20:1 (calculated by dividing the original image size by the size of the compressed image). The higher the quality, the lower the ratio, which affects playback speed. Higher ratios normally produce faster playback speeds. Most compression schemes produce ratios that depend on the image content (i.e. the more complex the image, the less compression you can expect).

Controller: A remote control device for synchronising and controlling several VCR decks while editing.

Development money: This is money allocated to the production team by the commissioning group/s in the very early stages of a project to produce a preliminary budget and script. Today, it is often also the case that production companies fund the initial development of up and coming projects from their 10–15% production fee.

Difference: A concept derived from new cultural politics whereby different racial, sexual and gender 'voices' are foregrounded to challenge the dominance of male bourgeois culture.

Digital: An adjective applied to any system which encodes, stores (as a series of 1's and 0's) and decodes audio or visual data within a computer or digital environment. The quality is generally higher than that of analogue systems of similar cost, and digital signals retain that quality through transmission, copying, et cetera.

Direct Cinema: A type of documentary practice championed by Robert Drew et al. in the 1960s whereby 'fly-on-the-wall' techniques – real time, long duration takes, avoidance of voice-over – attempt an objective, 'direct' record of the subject matter. Here, makers try to avoid conditioning the events.

Digitised: The capture or import of digital data into a computer environment and the conversion of analogue material to digital. The amount of data stored is dependent on compression, which is a technique that reduces the size of a saved file by eliminating redundancies or reducing the amount of information stored, subsequently affecting quality.

Documentary Features: In recent years more feature length documentaries have been made with an eye on theatrical runs and video/DVD releases. Often these films mimic the conventions of popular fiction films – e.g. genre conventions – to find favour with distributors and audiences.

Docu-soaps: A documentary format pioneered on TV in the 1970s, and very dominant today. Series are constructed around 'a small group of charismatic characters' all involved in 'a common endeavour' such as working at an airport, going on holiday, taking driving lessons etc.

DV/Beta/VHS: These are videotape formats: DV = Digital Video, Beta and VHS are analogue. The formats are usually differentiated by picture resolution (lines per frame) or difference in quality (professional versus domestic).

Dynamics of sound: The amount of volume or "level".

Emblematic: An image or sound that is representative of a concept or a film's overall thesis, such as the use of an establishing shot in order to determine context or genre.

Expositional: A form of address or strategy within documentary exploiting a rhetorical or explanatory approach to the subject matter, often presenting categories and analysis of material.

'Foley' work: the process whereby individuals in studios create sounds to match images of a motion picture.

Frame rate: The rate at which video is scanned, recorded or played back by the video equipment (the PAL system has 625 lines of information per frame, at 25 frames/sec).

Hard Drive: A large capacity digital storage device for computer and digitised audiovisual data.

Humanist: A doctrine which takes human experience as the starting point of knowledge.

Indexical: A term originating from linguistics, and here indicating an existential bond between the photographic image and the world it captures.

Informed Consent: This is a term used to describe a level of consent where social actors are fully aware of the consequences of their appearance on camera before they sign their release forms.

Intertextual: The term is used here to imply the complex web of generic relationships that exist within Big Brother, and the symbiotic, crossover relationships that exist between TV and new-media in this multimedia event.

Liberal: As used here, a term implying values such as tolerance, liberty, protection of minority rights and inclusivity.

Linear editing: An additive, tape based system of editing. New material can only be "inserted" earlier on the tape by copying over material already present.

'Multiple' Theatrical Run: This is where a film is shown simultaneously at a number of cinema 'screens'.

Mono: Monophonic recording or single channel sound.

Motif: A recurrent emblem, sound or image associated with a specific idea or theme.

Naturalism: An aesthetic which takes the form of detailed reportage and 'scientific' documentation in an attempt to achieve an objective record of reality. In documentary, it is typified by location shooting, natural light, long takes and so forth.

Non-diegetic sound: This refers to sound which does not originate or represent audio within the world of the narrative, such as music and special effects.

Non-linear editing: A digital, computer based system of editing which, like film editing, allows the editor to rearrange the edited sequences in any order after they have been laid down.

Offline: The rough cut of a video.

Online: The final edit of a video.

Pre-roll time: A predetermined unit of time which enables VCRs to rewind prior to the point of commitment for an edit in order to allow each machine to synchronise.

Pastiche: A term meaning an imitation of styles, without a sense of comic irony that you would associate with parody. Pastiche is a characteristic of the postmodern, whereas parody is often associated with a modernist, critical sensibility.

Performance: Makers of documentaries are only too aware of the potential effects of a camera and crew on social actors – provoking the unforeseen, illuminating a truth, stimulating deceptive performances, creating 'stars' etc. Docu-soaps opt very clearly for the latter, encouraging their social actors to perform on camera, often to a point of caricature. These 'stars' are built up through promotion and publicity to add entertainment value to the programme.

Reality TV: A term first coined in the early 1990s to describe actuality shows that present 'dangerous events, unusual situations, or actual police cases' (Nichols 1994: 45) – all to entertain audiences. Recently the term has been expanded to include human interest/ confessional genres.

Representation: When we film an event or persons, we need to be aware that our representations of them are never completely 'innocent' and are – to some degree at least – subject to existing cultural codes and conventions. As makers, the manner in which we position ourselves in relation to these codes is based on our ethical positions.

Rhetorical devices: These are cinematic formal devices – editing, *mise-en-scène* and sound – used to achieve a persuasive line of argument.

Social Actors: Those persons who appear in a documentary.

Streaming Media: A collection of technologies that allow the delivery of moving images across the internet, whereby video is highly compressed and delivered on demand to each viewer.

Subjectivity and Intent: Ethical makers foreground any intentions they may have so that viewers are aware of them. Subjective truths that are rigorously researched, well argued and provocative are the most non-fiction makers can achieve in their documentaries.

Timecode: A synchronisation system, assigning a corresponding hours/minutes/seconds/ frame number designation to every frame (25 frames/sec).

Tone of sound: The particular "timbre" of the sound, from a smooth to a rough texture.

Subsystems: Systems or structures of storytelling (or organisation of audiovisual material) which lie beneath the surface of the principal text or story, such as continuity, staging and editing. These systems are co-dependent, whether technical or aesthetic, and support the principal text and aid in its presentation and interpretation.

Symbolic: A term indicating meanings that are underlying, beyond mere visual resemblance, and are culturally determined.

Verisimilitude: The appearance of being true.

Vox pops: Meaning 'voice of the people'. A series of shots or 'pieces to camera' where a selection of the public are asked to comment on a question or issue as posited by the film-maker. This sequence is then often presented as representative of public opinion.

'Zebras': These are exposure indicators visible within the viewfinder of a camera. The zebra patterning becomes visible as a result of overexposure, which means that any detail in the overexposed area will be lost.

index